ABOUT THIS B

Have you ever looked into [   ] hat space is like? How big it is? Wha[   ]h may seem enormous, but it is min[   ]pace, also known as the universe. In fact, some astronomers and scientists have said that Earth looks like a tiny, pale blue dot from space. The universe is a huge open area that holds everything you could think of: planets, moons, stars, galaxies . . . and some of the greatest mysteries of all time.

In *Spaceopedia*, get ready to blast off on a tour of our amazing universe. Our first mission is to the night sky. On a clear night, you can see thousands of stars. And with the help of a telescope, you can see even farther into our galaxy. From the northern sky to the southern sky, we'll visit the marvels of the constellations.

Hold on tight, because once our adventure starts, you will quickly come face-to-face with the wild side of space. We'll take an in-depth look at the Sun, the Moon, and each planet of our Solar System. You'll learn about Jupiter's Great Red Spot, how Uranus got knocked on its side, and how mathematics led to Neptune's discovery. And from asteroids to comets speeding through the sky, we'll get to know some movers and shakers.

Our galaxy is called the Milky Way, and our closest star, the Sun, is just one of billions of stars. We will journey through the life cycle of a star and uncover the mystery of why stars twinkle so brightly. Then we'll enter deep space, where we'll find the strangest stuff of all. Finding out about black holes and the search for life on other planets will be our most exciting adventure yet.

How do scientists explore the universe? You'll learn about extraordinary NASA missions to space, find out how telescopes work, and meet some of the most important astronauts. You'll get an insider's view of what it's like to be an astronaut and work in the International Space Station (ISS), which travels in orbit above Earth.

Along the way, Hakeem Oluseyi will be your trusty guide. He's an astrophysicist—which means he's a space expert—and he has lots of experience observing the universe and explaining how it works. Throughout the book, check out "Ask Hakeem" to get all your questions answered.

You can read this book from front to back or dip in anywhere— every page is filled with fascinating facts about space and photos of its amazing objects. At the end, you'll find resources for learning more about space, including activities, science centers to visit, and more. Turn the page to start your journey into space.

Contents

About This Book 3
Introduction by astrophysicist Hakeem Oluseyi . . .6

OUR ADDRESS IN THE UNIVERSE 8

WHAT IS SPACE LIKE? 10

HOW LIGHT TRAVELS IN SPACE 12

IN THE NIGHT SKY 14

ASTRONOMY
Stargazing 16

CONSTELLATIONS
The Northern Sky .18
The Southern Sky .20

TELESCOPES
How Telescopes Work 22
Giant Telescopes .24

THE EARTH, MOON, AND SUN 26

THE SPIN ZONE
Earth's Orbit 28
Earth's Rotation 30
Earth's Tilt 32

EARTH'S MOON
The Moon 34
Phases of the Moon 36

ECLIPSES
What Is an Eclipse? 38

THE SUN
What Is the Sun? .40
Inside the Sun 42
Solar Activity 44

BLASTOFF!
How Rockets Launch 46
The Space Shuttle 48
Early Space Missions 50
The Moon Landing 52
Becoming an Astronaut 54

THE SOLAR SYSTEM 56

HOW THE SOLAR SYSTEM WORKS
Perfect Harmony .58
Great Discoveries .60
Birth of a Planet .62

TERRESTRIAL PLANETS
Mercury 64
Venus 66
Earth 68
Earth's Anatomy .70
Earth's Atmosphere 72
Mars 74
Is There Water on Mars? 76

ROBOTS IN SPACE
Missions to Mars .78

JOVIAN PLANETS
Jupiter 80
Jupiter's Moons 82
Saturn 84
Saturn's Rings 86
Uranus 88
Neptune 90

EXPLORATION
Missions to Outer Planets 92

LIFE IN SPACE
International Space Station 94
Daily Life at the ISS 96
Spacewalking 98
Microgravity 100
Space Experiments 102

ASTEROIDS, METEORS, COMETS AND MORE 104

ASTEROIDS
The Asteroid Belt 106

SPACE JUNK
Strange Debris .108

SHOOTING STARS
Meteors 110

IMPACT CRATERS
Meteorite Craters. .112

DWARF PLANETS
The Kuiper Belt. 114

COMETS
The Oort Cloud 116

ROSETTA MISSION
Landing on a Comet. 118

SUPER STARS. 120

HOW STARS EVOLVE
Star Qualities. 122
Life Cycle of a Star. 124

FORMING STARS
Nebulas. 126
Eagle Nebula 128

YOUNG STARS
Main Sequence Stars. 130

MATURE STARS
Giant Stars 132
Supergiant Stars .134

DYING STARS
Planetary Nebulas and White Dwarfs. 136
Supernovas. 138
Neutron Stars. 140
Black Holes. 142

STAR SYSTEMS
Binary Stars and Multistars. 144

THE SPECTRUM
Energy. 146
Invisible Energy 148
Measuring Energy in Space. 150

THE UNIVERSE BEYOND. 152

GALAXIES
What Is a Galaxy?. 154
The Milky Way. 156

The Galactic Core 158
The Local Group. .160
The Magellanic Cloud 162
Galaxy Clusters 164
Quasars. 166

MYSTERIES OF SPACE
Origins of the Universe 168
The Expanding Universe 170
The Fate of the Universe 172

SPACE EXPLORATION. 174

AMAZING IMAGES
The Hubble Space Telescope 176
Hubble Discoveries 178

RESEARCH
NASA 180

NEW FRONTIERS
Blast Off to Mars!. 182
Life Beyond Earth. 184
Future Space Exploration 186

Be a Space Explorer! 188
Photo Credits 190

Glittering stars

Jupiter's moon Io

ISS flyaround

Apollo 8's view of Earth

NGC 5189 nebula

Plasma eruptions on the Sun

Comet ISON

Whirlpool galaxy

I've always been a science guy, even from a young age. But it wasn't until I was 11 years old. That's when I started getting to know Albert Einstein's work, and I became really excited about science. It knocked my socks off! I did everything I could to get my head around his theories and what he wrote. My passion for physics grew—you could say it grew exponentially! In high school, I won a prize in a science competition. The judges saw potential in me and really encouraged me to follow the path to becoming a physicist.

After high school, I joined the military and from there I ventured on to Tougaloo College in Mississippi. While at Tougaloo, I was one of only two physics graduates. I entered the field of research at the University of Georgia and then went on to Stanford University and earned a PhD.

After graduate school, I worked on a project called the SuperNova/Acceleration Prove (SNAP) mission, a space-based telescope for observing supernovae at Lawrence Berkeley National Laboratory. The mission was awesome—we were able to observe thousands of supernovae per year and it helped us learn more about dark energy.

In addition to research and teaching, I've been involved with an organization called Cosmos Education whose mission is to bring science and technology education to underdeveloped countries. Cosmos Education performs science demonstrations for kids and discusses issues such as sustainable development within Africa, and I've visited schools in Africa, where I try to inspire young students to reach for the stars.

You may think of scientists as super-intellectual, but I'm just a regular guy, and I really like talking to students. What I want to do is help make learning science easy. People say I can take the most complicated science theory and explain it in a way that everyone can understand. My goal now is to do all I can to encourage young scientists to research and learn.

I hope *Spaceopedia* inspires you to learn more. Who knows, maybe one day you'll be a scientist, too!

Our Address in the Universe

Earth lives in a neighborhood, just like you do. Earth's neighborhood is known as the Solar System. While Earth doesn't have a street address, people often say Earth's location is the third planet from the Sun. Let's look at where we are before we start our amazing journey into space.

YOU ARE HERE: EARTH

Our planet, Earth, has just the right balance of elements to support life. We have enough water, land, air, and sunlight to survive, and an atmosphere to protect us. Earth has quite a few nicknames, including "the Big Blue Marble," "the Blue Planet," "the Water Planet," "Terra," and "the Third Rock from the Sun."

Jupiter

Mercury

Earth

Venus

Mars

AND HERE: THE SOLAR SYSTEM

The Earth and seven other planets all revolve around the Sun, making up the solar system. The inner planet family, known as the terrestrial planets, consists of Mercury, Venus, Earth, and Mars. The outer planet family, also called the Jovian planets or the gas giants, includes Jupiter, Saturn, Uranus, and Neptune.

AND ALSO HERE:
THE MILKY WAY

A galaxy is a large group of stars, dust, and gas. Our solar system is one small part of the Milky Way Galaxy. The galaxy was named the Milky Way because it has so many stars that it looks like a river of milk in the sky. The Milky Way is a spiral galaxy with two major arms, Scutum-Centaurus and Perseus, and several minor arms. The solar system that we belong to is on a minor arm called the Orion Arm.

Uranus

Neptune

Saturn

WAIT! HERE, TOO:
THE LOCAL GROUP

The Milky Way is part of a group of galaxies called the Local Group. Astronomers think there are more than 50 galaxies in the Local Group; among the biggest are the Milky Way and the Andromeda Galaxy.

What Is Space Like?

Beyond Earth is a place we call space, whose environment is very different from our planet's. Imagine that you are transported to space. The first thing you will notice is that you are weightless and floating around. It is completely silent.

At first, it will seem like you are surrounded by endless darkness. As your eyes adjust, you may see points of light in every direction—these are stars. You can look down and have a bird's-eye view of lightning storms happening on Earth.

ROLLER COASTER

EARTH GRAVITY VS. SPACE GRAVITY

Gravity is a force that pulls your body downward. When you drop something, gravity is what makes it fall. On Earth, gravity keeps everything that has weight from flying off into space. There is gravity in space, too! We know that because satellites and celestial objects stay in orbit.

Have you ever been on a roller coaster that suddenly drops? Can you remember what it feels like? This is called free fall, or weightlessness. This is the feeling you have when you and the object you are in are both falling together.

Have you seen astronauts bouncing around, weightless, inside their spacecraft? In space, the spacecraft and the astronauts are both falling around Earth together. This means that if something isn't held down, it doesn't stay put. Liquids, foods, tools, and even sleeping astronauts have to be strapped down to keep them from drifting away.

WEIGHTLESSNESS ON A SPACECRAFT

HOW MUCH WOULD YOU WEIGH IN SPACE?

Weight depends on the force of gravity on an object. If you travelled to a planet with more mass as Earth but the same size you would feel heavier because the gravity is stronger. On a planet with less mass, gravity is weaker and you'd feel lighter. Here is how much a 100-pound (45 kg) person would weigh on each planet.

WHY IS SPACE SO DARK?

Even though stars generate light, space is mostly dark, because there are empty areas where there is little to emit or reflect light. If you see a photo of Earth taken from space, Earth appears lit up because the Sun is reflecting its light onto the planet's surface.

WHY IS SPACE SO QUIET?

There is no air in space. Sound travels in waves that need air molecules in order to vibrate and create audible noises. If there is no air, there is no sound.

BY THE NUMBERS
GRAVITY

100
POUNDS ON EARTH
(45 kg)

76
POUNDS ON MERCURY
(34 kg)

181
POUNDS ON VENUS
(82 kg)

34
POUNDS ON THE MOON
(15 kg)

76
POUNDS ON MARS
(34 kg)

473
POUNDS ON JUPITER
(215 kg)

178
POUNDS ON SATURN
(81 kg)

473
POUNDS ON URANUS
(215 kg)

224
POUNDS ON NEPTUNE
(102 kg)

How Light Travels in Space

Light is the fastest thing there is. If you could travel at the speed of light, you could zip around Earth 7.5 times in just one second. That's pretty amazing, since it would take the fastest airplane 67 hours to travel around the world only once! The speed of light in a vacuum—that is, with nothing in its path—is 186,282 miles per second (299,792 kps).

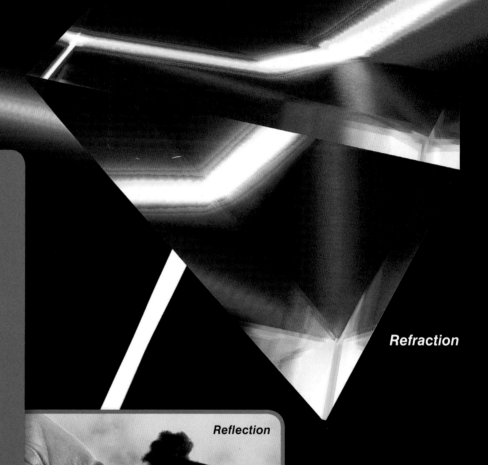

Refraction

Reflection

CHANGING DIRECTION

Light travels in waves and particles, and it can be slowed down if it comes in contact with an object or dust in space. When sunlight reaches Earth's atmosphere, it can enter in different ways. Light can be reflected off clouds or Earth's surface. It can also be scattered in the atmosphere through refraction.

Reflection is affected by how smooth the surface is. You can see how this works by looking into still water. The image you see reflected will be clear. If you throw a stone in the water, ripples form. The light bounces off the ripples and your reflection won't be clear. You can see this in the image at right.

Refraction happens when light scatters. A change in speed effects the direction of refracted light when it hits an object. If you shine light into water, or through a piece of glass or plastic, the light slows down and bends. You can see this in the prism shown to the right.

GALACTIC FACT

When a ray of white light hits a glass prism at an angle, the light refracts, revealing a group of visible colors: red, orange, yellow, green, blue, indigo, and violet. More than 300 years ago, physicist Sir Isaac Newton discovered that white light consists of all these colors, debunking the belief at the time that the prism added the colors.

ASK HAKEEM...

WHY IS THE SKY BLUE?

The atmosphere is a mixture of gas molecules that surrounds Earth. As light moves through the atmosphere, its longer wavelengths (like red, orange, yellow, etc.) pass straight through. But, a shorter wavelength (blue!) is absorbed by the gas molecules. The absorbed blue light then is radiated in different directions and scattered all around the sky.

MEASURING DISTANCE IN SPACE

Astronomers use light-years instead of miles to measure distances in space. Light-years tell us how long it takes for light from an object in space to reach Earth. One light-year equals 5,880,000,000,000 miles (9,462,942,720,000 km). The farther away a celestial object is, the longer its light takes to get to Earth. When you see sunlight, it is already 8 minutes and 20 seconds old. That's how long it takes for light from the Sun to reach Earth. And believe it or not, that's pretty quick. Here are times it takes light to travel to Earth from different places in space.

BY THE NUMBERS
LIGHT-YEARS

1.3
LIGHT-SECONDS
The Moon

8:20
LIGHT-MINUTES
The Sun

4
LIGHT-HOURS
Neptune

4.3
LIGHT-YEARS
Proxima Centauri

AT A GLANCE

ASTRONOMY

Astronomy is the scientific study of things beyond Earth's atmosphere, including stars, planets, and much more.

THE CONSTELLATIONS

➡ Notable constellations and asterisms include:

- Ursa Major and the Big Dipper*
- Canis Major (The Dog Star)
- Virgo
- Cassiopeia
- Hydra
- Orion
- Crux
- The Southern Cross*

TELESCOPES

➡ Help us see faraway things up close

➡ Have special lenses and mirrors

➡ Giant telescopes can be as large as a building and let scientists look even farther into space

*An asterism

WORD

An **asterism** is a smaller group of stars that form a pattern we can recognize in the night sky. Constellations are based on asterisms and we can see asterisms inside constellations.

In the Night Sky

When you look up at the night sky, what do you see? In ancient times, people thought that the Moon and stars were gods moving across the sky. In about 600 BCE, Thales, a Greek astronomer, suggested that Earth was a round ball, not a god. He also believed the Moon was bright because the Sun reflected light onto it. It was from this point in history that humans began to describe nature with natural laws instead of mythology.

Today, we know so much more about what's beyond Earth. And you can study it, too. Go outside on a clear night and you will get the best view. Depending on the season and your location, you will be able to see thousands of stars, some planets, and many constellations.

A constellation is a region of the sky that includes a group of stars that are in a shape or pattern. Many years ago, in ancient civilizations, people noticed that some star patterns resembled animals and mythological characters, such as Orion the Hunter. In the past, constellations were used as maps for travelers. For example, they helped sailors navigate at sea, guiding them to their destinations. Today, we use them to help us find other objects in the sky, like planets.

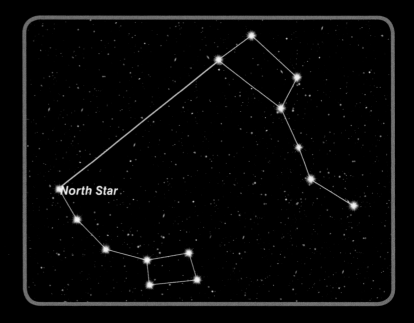

North Star

BY THE NUMBERS
THE NIGHT SKY

88
CONSTELLATIONS
in the night sky

5
PLANETS
you can see with your naked eye:
Mercury, Venus, Mars, Jupiter, and Saturn

20
MOONS
you can see with a telescope

WHAT CAN YOU SEE FROM YOUR BACKYARD?

The first celestial object you will notice is the Moon. Looking with just your eyes, you can see the craters on the Moon.

You can also see many constellations and asterisms. Look for a group of stars that looks like a soup ladle. Count seven stars. That's the Big Dipper.

To find the Little Dipper, use the Big Dipper as a guide. Look at the stars in the Big Dipper that are farthest away from the handle—some call them the pointers, because they point to Polaris, the North Star. The North Star is the last star in the handle of the Little Dipper.

There are five planets you can see with your naked eye: Mercury, Venus, Mars, Jupiter, and Saturn. They look like bright stars in the sky, but they don't seem to twinkle. This is because they are relatively close to Earth. You can see them most of the time during the year, except for short periods when they are closer to the Sun.

WHAT CAN YOU SEE WITH A TELESCOPE?

With a very simple telescope, you will be able to see even more, like the faraway planets Uranus and Neptune and the dwarf planet Pluto. A telescope will show you all the moons of Jupiter, Saturn, and Neptune, and you may even see some asteroids. Each time you look through a telescope, you are connecting to a part of the universe.

ASK HAKEEM...

WHY DO STARS TWINKLE?

Stars don't actually twinkle, they just look like they do. Stars are so far away from us, we can only see them as points of light. In the night sky, we are looking at them through very thick layers of moving air in Earth's atmosphere. As starlight travels through the atmosphere, the light is bent (refracted). The refraction "moves" the image around a tiny area and causes us to perceive the star as twinkling.

The Northern Sky

The entire sky is divided up into 88 regions. These are based on groupings of bright stars called asterisms, although most of us still call them constellations. Some are only visible from the Northern Hemisphere, some are only visible from the Southern Hemisphere, and some are visible from both hemispheres. In addition to your location, Earth's orbit and changing seasons also determine what we see. Some constellations are overhead all the time—these are called circumpolar.

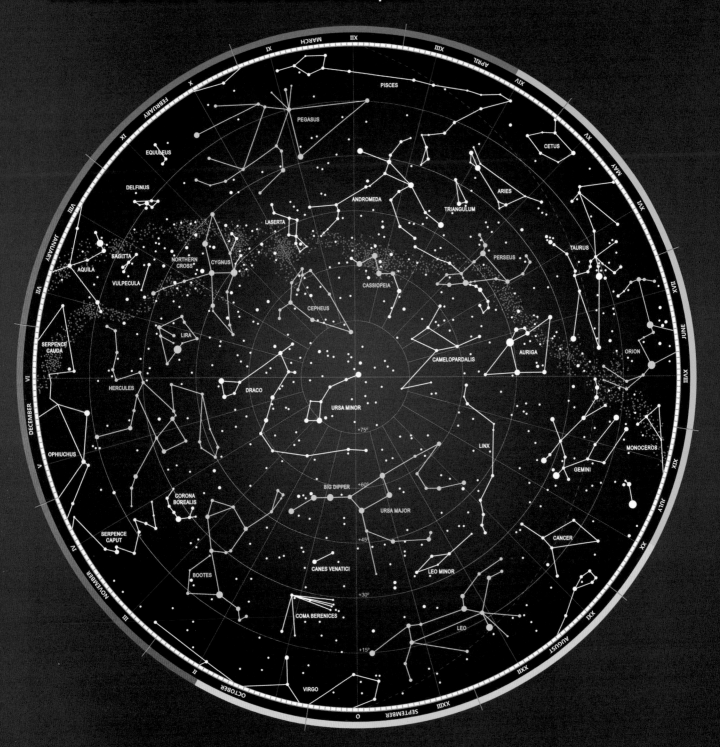

WHAT TO SPY IN THE SKY:

Can you spot these constellations in the star map on the left?

YEAR-ROUND:
Cepheus, Cassiopeia, Ursa Major

SPRING:
Boötes, Leo

SUMMER:
Hercules, Cygnus

FALL:
Pegasus, Lyra

WINTER:
Perseus, Orion (partial)

NORTHERN CROSS

The Northern Cross is part of the Cygnus constellation and includes the stars Deneb and Albireo. It marks a spot where the edge of the Milky Way is sometimes visible.

URSA MAJOR
(The Great Bear)

Ursa Major was one of the original constellations noted by famous ancient astronomer Ptolemy. It is one of the oldest and most famous patterns in the sky.

THE BIG DIPPER

The Big Dipper is a cluster of stars within Ursa Major. The stars in the Big Dipper are Alkaid, Mizar, Alioth, Megrez, Phecda, Merak, and Dubhe.

WORD

A **hemisphere** is half a sphere. Earth is divided into the Northern and Southern Hemispheres by the equator.

CASSIOPEIA

In Greek mythology, Cassiopeia was the wife of King Cepheus. She bragged that her daughter, Andromeda, was more beautiful than the gods. The gods were angry and sentenced Andromeda to be sacrificed to Cetus, a sea monster, but Perseus saved her. Cassiopeia, Cepheus, Andromeda, Cetus, and Perseus are all represented in the sky as constellations.

The Southern Sky

From the Southern Hemisphere, you can see the constellation Crux, which includes the asterism the Southern Cross, above the horizon all year round. The southern sky is also home to Sagittarius, which is a large constellation with many star clusters you can see with the help of binoculars or a telescope. From winter to spring, you can also see the two beautiful Magellanic Clouds. These are the two largest satellite galaxies of the Milky Way. Scientists have discovered more than 30 dwarf galaxies orbiting the Milky Way and believe there are likely many more to be discovered.

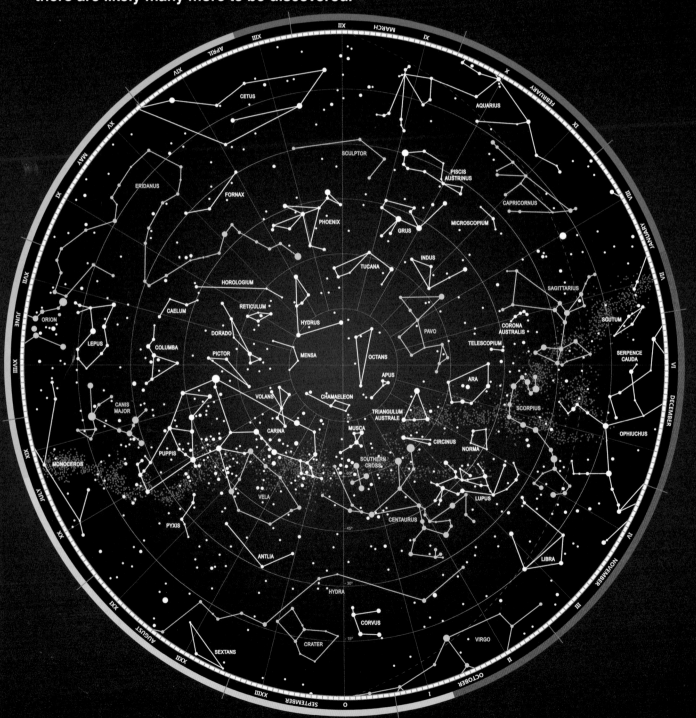

WHAT TO SPY IN THE SKY:

Can you spot these constellations in the star map on the left?

YEAR-ROUND:
Centaurus, Southern Cross, Pavo

SPRING:
Capricornus, Sculptor

SUMMER:
Eridanus, Vela, Orion (partial)

FALL:
Crater, Virgo (partial)

WINTER:
Sagittarius, Scorpius

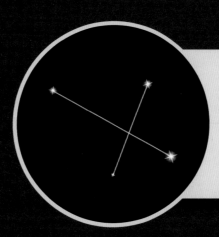

THE SOUTHERN CROSS

The best-known asterism in the southern sky is the Southern Cross. The star to look for in this constellation is Acrux, also called Alpha Crucis. It is a blue-white star that sits at the bottom of the cross.

CANIS MAJOR AND SIRIUS (The Dog Star)

Canis Major means "the great dog." It includes Sirius, the brightest star in the sky. Sirius is actually a double star. The companion star is named Sirius B, nicknamed the Pup.

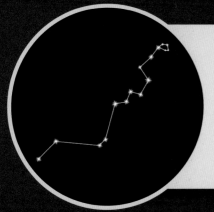

HYDRA

Hydra, shaped like a serpent, is the longest constellation. Mythology tells us that when Hercules cut off the Hydra's head, many more heads grew in its place.

DID YOU KNOW?

Orion is one of the largest constellations in the sky and is one of the easiest to find. It can be seen in the southern summer sky or the northern winter sky.

ORION

This constellation was named for the mythological Orion, a hunter in love with the goddess Artemis. But Artemis's brother Apollo did not like Orion. One day, Apollo bet Artemis that she could not hit an object in the distance with her bow and arrow. Artemis could not see that it was Orion, and she shot him. When she saw what she had done, she honored Orion by putting him in the stars. To spot this constellation, look for three bright stars in a straight line. These represent Orion's belt.

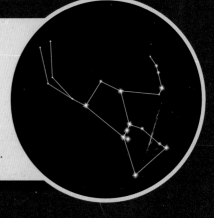

How Telescopes Work

The telescope was invented more than 400 years ago, and it changed the world of astronomy forever. A telescope improves your vision so that you can see faraway things up close. Let's say you want to look at the Moon. A telescope lens takes in more light from the Moon and magnifies it—spreading it over a larger area on the back of your eye—so you can see more detail.

REFRACTING TELESCOPES

All telescopes have pieces that work together to help you see objects in the night sky.

There is a lens at the bottom of a refracting telescope. This lens gathers the light coming from the object you want to see and sends it up the telescope's tube to the lens inside the eyepiece. The eyepiece enlarges the image so you can see it, like a magnifying glass would.

Galileo Galilei, an Italian astronomer who was born in the 1500s, developed a refracting telescope with two small lenses that fit into wooden tubes. It used a convex objective lens and a concave eyepiece lens.

PARTS OF A REFRACTING TELESCOPE

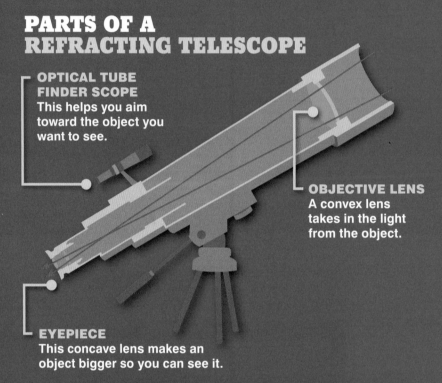

OPTICAL TUBE FINDER SCOPE
This helps you aim toward the object you want to see.

OBJECTIVE LENS
A convex lens takes in the light from the object.

EYEPIECE
This concave lens makes an object bigger so you can see it.

THE FIRST STEP

Hans Lippershey (1570–1619), a German-Dutch master lens grinder and spectacle maker, is credited with inventing the telescope. There is some controversy here: At the time, both Lippershey and Zacharias Janssen were creating optical lenses in the same town in the Netherlands. But Lippershey was the first to apply for a patent for his design of the 3x magnification telescope, "for seeing things far away as if they were nearby." However, it is unclear if he ever actually built a telescope.

HIGHLIGHTS FROM HISTORY: TELESCOPES

1608
Hans Lippershey was the first person to apply for a patent for a telescope.

1609 ▶
Galileo Galilei built a high-quality telescope and in 1610 discovered the moons around Jupiter.

Galileo demonstrates telescope

1611
Johannes Kepler wrote that a telescope should be built using two convex lenses.

1783 ▶
Caroline Herschel used a telescope to discover three new nebulae and a few years later found eight new comets.

Caroline Herschel at work

REFLECTING TELESCOPES

A reflecting telescope uses two mirrors instead of a lens. Light from an object enters the telescope's tube and is reflected off a curved mirror at the end of the tube. A second mirror inside the tube reflects the light to the eyepiece.

PARTS OF A REFLECTING TELESCOPE

EYEPIECE
A magnifying lens is used to view the image closely.

SECONDARY MIRROR
Another mirror, small and flat, moves the light to the best spot for focusing.

PRIMARY MIRROR
This mirror gathers and focuses light.

DID YOU KNOW?

A convex lens is curved outward and is thicker in the middle. When rays of light pass through, they are brought closer together, making an object look larger. A magnifying glass is an example of a convex lens.

A concave lens is curved inward and is thinner in the middle. When rays of light pass through, they are spread farther apart, making an object appear brighter.

Convex Lens   **Concave Lens**

1785-1789
William Herschel, who discovered Uranus, created a 47-inch (119 cm) reflecting telescope.

1917 ▶
In Pasadena, California, the Hooker Telescope allowed more discoveries in the Milky Way.

The Hale Telescope atop Mt. Palomar

1948
The 200-inch (5.1m) Hale Telescope opened on Palomar Mountain, California and continues to make discoveries to this day.

1990 ▶
The Hubble Space Telescope was launched into space by the space shuttle Discovery.

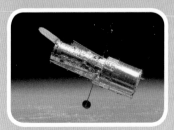

The Hubble Telescope in space

Giant Telescopes

Some telescopes are small enough to sit on your desk, and others are the size of buildings. It is these giant telescopes that probe the deepest, darkest secrets of the universe. Giant telescopes are so powerful that they may tell astronomers how the universe began.

SOUTHERN AFRICAN LARGE TELESCOPE (SALT)

LOCATION: SOUTH AFRICAN ASTRONOMICAL OBSERVATORY SUTHERLAND, SOUTH AFRICA

SALT is the largest single optical telescope in the Southern Hemisphere. It was built in a small village so that it would be far from city lights. Because this telescope is south of the equator, it has a fantastic view of the southern sky. The Large and Small Magellanic Clouds are easily viewed, as well as the center of the Milky Way Galaxy.

KECK I AND KECK II

LOCATION: W. M. KECK OBSERVATORY MAUNA KEA, HAWAII

When studying space, it helps to have the high ground! In the 1990s, these two telescopes were built on Mauna Kea, a dormant volcano, at an elevation of 13,600 feet (4,145 m). Scientists felt that this was a good location since it is always clear and dry there, ideal for observation. These telescopes are still among the largest in the world, with mirrors that are 33 feet (10 m) across.

Naked eye

Keck telescope

HOBBY-EBERLY TELESCOPE (HET)

LOCATION: MCDONALD OBSERVATORY FORT DAVIS, TEXAS

This giant telescope has unique large hexagon-shaped mirrors that help it gather more light. Its latest project, called HETDEX, will collect information from 1 million galaxies to study dark energy, thought to be why the universe is expanding.

GRAN TELESCOPIO CANARIAS (GTC)

LOCATION: OBSERVATORIO DEL ROQUE DE LOS MUCHACHOS LA PALMA, CANARY ISLANDS

Surpassing the size of Keck I and Keck II is the Gran Telescopio Canarias—the world's largest optical telescope. If you laid the Statue of Liberty on the telescope's mirror, the mirror would be almost as long! Located in the Canary Islands of Spain, the telescope was completed in 2009. Scientists hope to use the telescope to study the insides of black holes and learn more about how the universe began.

BY THE NUMBERS

THE 5 BIGGEST TELESCOPES

34
FEET (10.4 m)
Gran Telescopio
Canarias, Canary
Islands, Spain

33
FEET (10 m)
Keck I, Mauna Kea,
Hawaii

33
FEET (10 m)
Keck II, Mauna Kea,
Hawaii

30
FEET (9.1 m)
Southern African Large
Telescope, Sutherland,
South Africa

30
FEET (9.1 m)
Hobby-Eberly
Telescope,
Fort Davis, Texas

AT A GLANCE

EARTH'S ORBIT
➡ Earth orbits the Sun in an oval path.
➡ It takes Earth one year to revolve around the Sun.

EARTH'S ROTATION
➡ Earth spins on its axis.
➡ Daytime is when the side of Earth you're on is turned toward the Sun.
➡ Nighttime is when the side of Earth you're on is turned away from the Sun.

EARTH'S TILT
➡ We have seasons thanks to Earth's tilt.
➡ But if you live at the equator, you have no seasons.

THE MOON
➡ The Moon is Earth's only natural satellite.
➡ There are eight phases of the Moon.

ECLIPSES
➡ A solar eclipse happens when the Moon passes in a direct line between Earth and the Sun.
➡ A lunar eclipse occurs when the Moon passes through Earth's shadow.

THE SUN
➡ Is an ordinary yellow dwarf star.
➡ Is 4.5 billion years old.

The Earth, Moon, and Sun

Earth, the Moon, and the Sun are always in motion, making life on Earth possible. Without the Moon, our ocean's tides would change. And without the Sun, we would have no warmth. The Sun would speed away in its motion about the galaxy and Earth would be left in cold darkness.

Earth's Orbit

Earth revolves around the Sun on an invisible path called an orbit. The shape of this path is oval, not round, so scientists call it an elliptical orbit. Because of this oval shape, the distance between Earth and the Sun changes throughout the year.

THREE REVOLUTIONARY THEORIES

Is Earth or the Sun at the center of our solar system? Long ago, astronomers first attempted to answer this question.

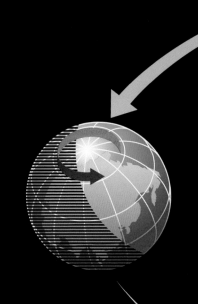

About 150 CE, astronomer Ptolemy recorded the theory that everything in our solar system revolved around Earth. This is known as the geocentric theory. Though incorrect, it seems to makes sense, because when we look in the sky, it appears that the Sun and stars are moving.

In the early 1500s, Nicolaus Copernicus discovered that our Sun was the center of the solar system. He theorized that all the planets in the solar system, including Earth, were rotating around the Sun. This is true, and is called the heliocentric theory.

Tycho Brahe was born a few years after Copernicus's death. He studied the Moon and Mars and analyzed how planets moved. He thought that Earth stood still at the center of the solar system and the Sun and Moon revolved around Earth, while the other planets revolved around the Sun.

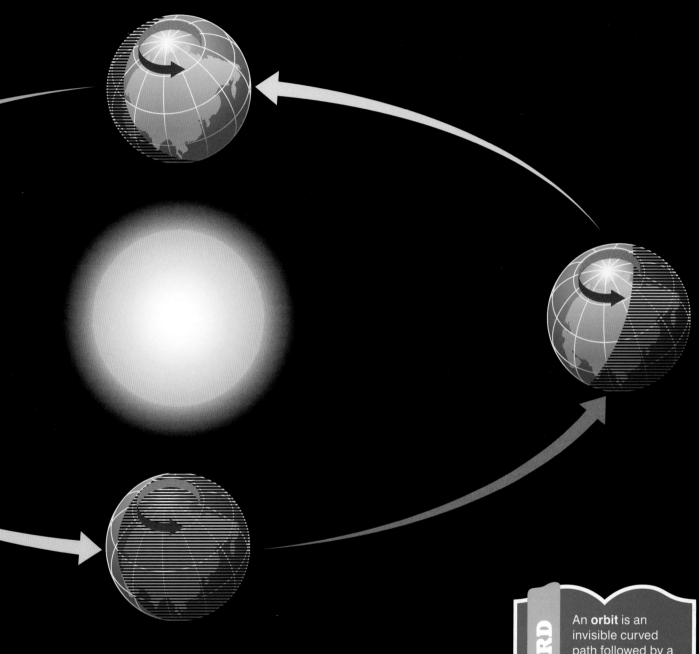

GALACTIC FACT

It takes Earth 365.25 days to make one complete revolution around the Sun. It moves around the Sun at a whopping 67,000 miles per hour (107,826 kph).

WORD

An **orbit** is an invisible curved path followed by a planet, satellite, or spaceship around a celestial body.

Earth's Rotation

Not only is Earth traveling in a path around the Sun, it is also slowly spinning at all times. Earth's spin is called rotation.

A SMOOTH RIDE

If Earth is spinning constantly, why aren't we dizzy? The Earth rotates at 1,000 miles (1,609 km) an hour, but because it never slows down or speeds up, we can't feel the spin. It's similar to being in a moving car, bus, or train: As long as it is moving at a steady speed, you aren't aware of the movement. It's only when the vehicle speeds up or slows down that you can feel it.

WORD

Earth rotates on its **axis**. Imagine an invisible line between the North and South Poles. That imaginary line is called Earth's axis.

GALACTIC FACT

It takes 24 hours for planet Earth to complete one rotation on its axis.

DAY AND NIGHT

When your day starts, the Sun appears to rise in the east. Then, when the Sun sets, it appears to go down in the west. But the Sun isn't moving. It's Earth that is. When the place where you are on the globe is closer to the Sun, it's daytime. When it's farther away, it's nighttime. The Sun looks like it is moving because Earth is rotating on its axis.

THINGS THAT SPIN

HULA HOOP

PINWHEEL

BLENDER

TOP

MERRY-GO-ROUND

Earth's Tilt

As Earth orbits the Sun, its axis is on a tilt. Think of Earth as leaning just a bit (as if you were drinking from a water fountain). Scientists believe that long, long ago, something hit Earth and knocked it so that it doesn't spin straight up and down. Earth's tilt causes the seasons.

WHY DO WE HAVE SEASONS?

Earth's tilt makes the North Pole point either toward or away from the Sun at different times of the year.

When the northern part of Earth leans toward the Sun, it gets more sunshine, which means longer days and higher temperatures. Simultaneously, the southern half of Earth leans away from the Sun. Less time facing the Sun means shorter, colder days and lower temperatures. Because Earth's tilt doesn't change, six months later, the northern half of Earth points away, and the seasons are reversed.

DECEMBER
➡ Summer south of the equator, winter north of the equator

MARCH
➡ Fall south of the equator, spring north of the equator

JUNE
➡ Winter south of the equator, summer north of the equator

SEPTEMBER
➡ Spring south of the equator, fall north of the equator

DECEMBER IN AUSTRALIA

DECEMBER IN CANADA

WHAT IF...
YOU LIVE AT THE EQUATOR?

If you live in a country at the equator, like Ecuador or Uganda, there are no seasons. It's because the Sun always strikes the equator at the same angle. The equator gets 12 hours of sunlight every single day.

WHAT IF...
YOU LIVED AT THE NORTH OR SOUTH POLE?

The North Pole and South Pole remain cold because they are never tilted into the direct path of the Sun. During the middle of winter, when a pole is tilted away from the Sun, it's always dark out, because the Sun never rises. During the middle of summer, the poles receive only sunlight, and there is no nighttime.

GALACTIC FACT

The axis of planet Earth is tilted about 23 to 26 degrees.

Summer   *Winter*

▶ The sun rising at the South Pole in September. It will not set for another six months until the summer solstice in December.

SUMMER SOLSTICE

Every year, on or around June 21, the North Pole is turned most toward the Sun. We call this the summer solstice, the longest day of the year in the Northern Hemisphere.

WINTER SOLSTICE

The shortest day of the year is when the North Pole is turned farthest from the Sun. Occuring on or around December 21, this is known as the winter solstice.

How was the Moon created? Scientists believe that it was created when another planet hit Earth so hard that the debris from Earth was sent into orbit. The rocky debris orbited Earth and eventually was pulled together by gravity, creating the Moon.

STELLAR STATS
THE MOON

DIAMETER
➡ 2,160 miles (3,476 km)

MASS
➡ 1.2 percent of Earth's mass

AVERAGE DISTANCE FROM EARTH
➡ 238,855 miles (384,400 km)

TIME FOR ONE ROTATION
➡ 27 Earth days

TIME TO ORBIT EARTH
➡ 27 Earth days

GRAVITY
➡ One-sixth as strong as gravity on Earth

TEMPERATURE FACING THE SUN
➡ 250°F (121°C)

TEMPERATURE ON THE DARK SIDE
➡ –243°F (–153°C)

WORD

A **satellite** is something orbiting or moving around another object. There are natural satellites, like moons, as well as man-made satellites that we've put in orbit.

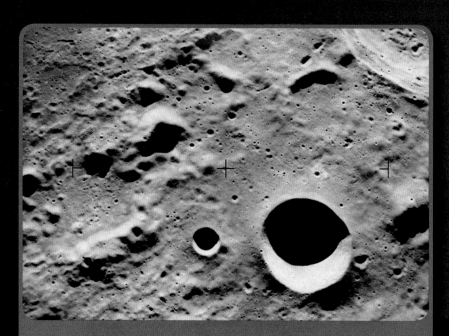

THE MOON UP CLOSE

Over billions of years, the Moon has been hit by many rocky bodies. If you look at the Moon through a telescope, you'll notice a lot of craters—proof of those collisions. Because the Moon does not have a special layer of moving plates on its surface like Earth does, it gets damaged. It cannot "heal" its outer layer.

WHAT IF ... THE MOON DISAPPEARED?

Without the Moon, Earth would not be the same. Our beautiful night sky would be without moonlight. Here are two more things that would change:

SMALLER TIDES

The ocean tides are affected by the Sun and the Moon. Without the gravitational pull from the Moon, the tides would be smaller.

WHY IS THE MOON SO BRIGHT?

The Moon is Earth's only natural satellite, and while it's the brightest object in our sky, it doesn't create any light of its own. The reason we see it so brightly is because our Sun shines on it at night.

A WOBBLY WORLD

Scientists believe that the Moon acts as a shock absorber to Earth and provides stability. If the Moon were to disappear, Earth might wobble more. Without the Moon, Earth might rotate faster, winds might kick up, and our atmosphere would change—creating extreme climates in all areas of the world.

Each month, the Moon goes through cycles you can see, called phases. Just as people long ago used the stars to navigate, early civilizations watched the phases of the Moon to mark the passage of time. It was the first calendar.

THE MANY PHASES OF THE MOON

What we call moonlight is really sunlight reflecting from the Moon. The Sun always illuminates half the Moon's orb. The fraction of the illuminated side that we see tells us which phase we are seeing.

During the eight phases of the Moon, which cycle over about four weeks, the Moon's position relative to Earth and the Sun is always changing as the Moon travels around Earth. Why do we always see the same side of the Moon? The Moon rotates on its axis, and this takes about the same amount of time as it does to orbit Earth.

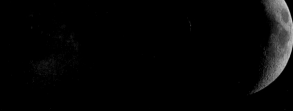

NEW MOON
The new Moon is the phase in which the Moon passes directly between the Sun and Earth. The illuminated side of the Moon is completely hidden from Earth, and we cannot see it.

WAXING CRESCENT
The waxing crescent phase is called a young Moon. It can be seen in the west after sunset.

FIRST QUARTER
This is the third phase of the Moon. People on Earth can see half the Moon's illuminated side.

WAXING GIBBOUS
Waxing means that the Moon is moving towards a full Moon, and gibbous means that more than half is illuminated.

▶ FULL AND BRIGHT

The full Moon that is closest to the autumnal equinox is called a Harvest Moon. In a time before electricity and tractor lights, this bright moon gave farmers extra time to harvest their crops.

WORD

The word **month** comes from the word *Moon*. The Moon orbits Earth once a month.

FULL MOON

When Earth is between the Sun and the Moon, we see the entire illuminated side of the Moon. This is when the Moon is brightest in the sky.

WANING GIBBOUS

Waning means that the moon is moving toward a new Moon. At this phase, it is more than half full.

LAST QUARTER

About one week after a full Moon, we can see only half the Moon's illuminated side.

WANING CRESCENT

This is the final sliver of the Moon that can be seen before the illuminated side of the Moon is completely hidden from us.

An eclipse occurs when one object gets between you and another object and blocks your view. There are two kinds of eclipses: solar, when the Sun is blocked from view, and lunar, when the Moon is blocked from view.

SOLAR ECLIPSE

A solar eclipse happens when the Moon passes in a direct line between Earth and the Sun. The Moon's shadow goes across Earth's surface and blocks out the sunlight.

➡ **Total Solar Eclipse:**
The Moon completely covers the view of the Sun. It's super dark.

➡ **Annular Solar Eclipse:**
The Moon covers the Sun's center, leaving the Sun's edges visible. It looks like a ring of fire.

➡ **Partial Solar Eclipse:**
The Moon only partially covers the disk of the Sun.

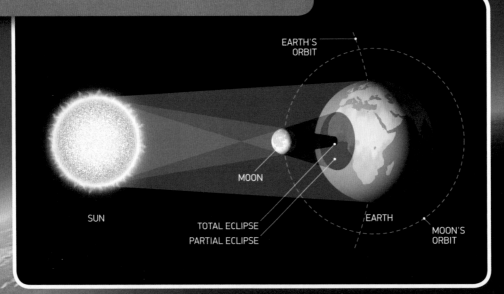

EARTH'S ORBIT

MOON

SUN

TOTAL ECLIPSE
PARTIAL ECLIPSE

EARTH

MOON'S ORBIT

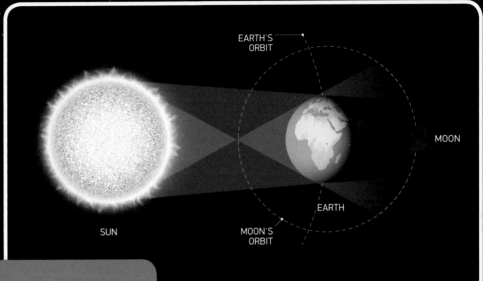

EARTH'S ORBIT

MOON

EARTH

SUN

MOON'S ORBIT

LUNAR ECLIPSE

A lunar eclipse happens when the Moon passes through Earth's shadow. A lunar eclipse can happen only during a full Moon. And a total lunar eclipse can happen only when the Sun, Moon, and Earth are in perfect alignment.

Lunar eclipses are not completely dark. The Moon will reflect some sunlight that is refracted by the atmosphere of Earth. Sometimes the Moon will look red. This is because light that is refracted is red in color.

A lunar eclipse can be seen by a much larger area of Earth than a solar eclipse.

➡ **Penumbral Lunar Eclipse:**
   This occurs when the outer shadow of Earth falls on the face of the Moon.

➡ **Umbral Lunar Eclipse:**
   The same as a total lunar eclipse in which the Moon is completely immersed in the umbra of Earth's shadow. (An umbra is a fully shaded area of a shadow cast by an opaque object.)

BY THE NUMBERS
ECLIPSES

7.5
MINUTES
The longest time a solar eclipse can last

5
THE MAXIMUM NUMBER
of solar eclipses that can occur on Earth within one year

4
THE MINIMUM NUMBER
of lunar and solar eclipses (two of each) that happen every year, though there can be more

What Is the Sun?

The sun is a yellow dwarf star. It is our nearest star, and it warms Earth, the oceans, and the atmosphere. It is the center of our Solar System, and its largest object. For humans, the Sun is the most important star in the universe; without it, Earth could not exist.

STELLAR STATS
THE SUN

DIAMETER
➡ 865,000 miles (1,392,080 km)

MASS
➡ 333,000 times Earth's mass

AVERAGE DISTANCE FROM EARTH
➡ 92,960,000 miles (149,604,618 km)

AGE
➡ 4.5 billion years old

SURFACE TEMPERATURE
➡ 10,000°F (5,538°C)

CORE TEMPERATURE
➡ 28,000,000°F (15,555,538°C)

READY FOR YOUR CLOSE-UP?

From a distance, the Sun seems bright and shiny. But the Sun's surface actually has a grainy appearance, which is called solar granulation. This happens because the Sun is completely covered by a boiling ocean of plasma. The hot plasma rises to the surface, where it cools and then descends again into the Sun's interior. These rising and falling regions are the granulation.

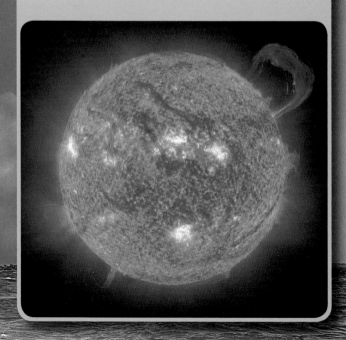

GALACTIC FACT

The Sun is so big that over a million Earths could fit inside it.

WHAT IS THE SUN MADE OF?

The Sun is primarily made of hydrogen and helium gas. Scientists have learned that the Sun started as a large, rotating cloud of gas called a solar nebula. The nebula collapsed due to gravity and began to spin more and more rapidly. Today, scientists regularly observe other stars and planetary systems forming in this same way.

HOW DOES THE SUN HELP EARTH?

The Sun warms Earth, the oceans, and the atmosphere.

Plants use a process called photosynthesis to harness energy from the Sun so they can grow.

The Sun is responsible for our weather. Our climates are dependent upon solar radiation from the Sun.

The energy we get from fossil fuels like oil originally came from the Sun.

We can use solar cells to convert energy from the Sun directly into electricity.

The Sun is a ball of hot plasma, and we know we cannot fly there because humans and rockets cannot withstand that heat. The Sun is so hot, it could easily melt steel. And since the Sun is gas, not solid, there would be no place to land. But we know a lot about the Sun without visiting it.

LAYERS OF THE SUN

1. CORONA
The outermost layer of the Sun is called the corona. This layer extends outward for millions of miles near the Sun and is up to 2,000,000°F (1,111,093°C). The corona releases gases that drift into space as solar winds at a speed of 500 miles per hour (805 kPH).

4. CONVECTIVE ZONE
This is a zone of boiling, bubbling plasma that moves energy outward through a process called convection.

2. CHROMOSPHERE
The chromosphere is the second of three layers of the Sun's atmosphere. It has an orange-red color. Temperatures here vary from 10,850°F to 36,035°F (6,000°C to 20,000°C).

5. RADIATIVE ZONE
In this zone, energy moves slowly outward. It takes about 170,000 years for energy to radiate through this layer of the Sun.

3. PHOTOSPHERE
The Sun's surface is called the photosphere, and its temperature is about 10,000°F (5,538°C). This is where sunspots appear.

6. CORE
This is where hydrogen is converted into helium. Because thermonuclear fusion is happening in this layer and gravity is placing pressure in the middle of the Sun, the core reaches an incredible 28,000,000°F (15,555,538°C).

HOW HOT IS IT?

82°F (28°C)
Average swimming pool temperature

98.6°F (37°C)
Temperature of the human body

500–700°F (260–371°C)
Burning charcoal in a grill

1,500–2,000°F (816–1,093°C)
Lava erupting from a volcano

10,800°F (5,982°C)
Earth's core

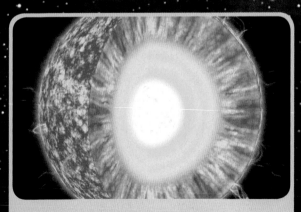

28,000,000°F (15,555,538°C)
Sun's core

Solar Activity

The Sun is a very active star. It's full of energy. In addition to the reactions going on in the core, much of the energy comes from activity on the Sun's surface, the solar cycle: sunspots, solar flares, and solar winds.

SUNSPOTS

Sunspots are regions on the surface of the Sun that appear darker. They look dark because they are cooler than other parts of the Sun. Although most of the Sun's surface is about 10,000°F (5,538°C), a large sunspot may be as "cold" as 5,700°F (3,149°C). Sometimes sunspots explode like volcanoes. Scientists call the eruptions solar storms. These storms release stored energy from inside the Sun.

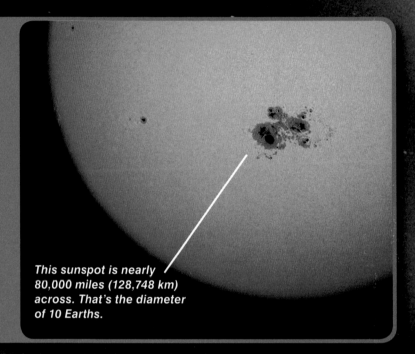

This sunspot is nearly 80,000 miles (128,748 km) across. That's the diameter of 10 Earths.

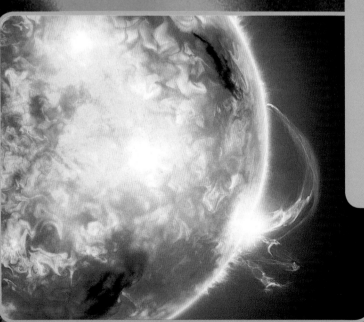

FLARIN' UP

There are frequently violent explosions on the Sun's surface. Solar flares occur when energy stored in the Sun's magnetic fields—an area where there are magnetic forces—gets transferred to the plasma at the Sun's surface.

SOLAR WINDS

When eruptions occur on the Sun, they cause gases and particles to be released into space. This sends tiny particles known as solar wind into the Solar System.

THE NORTHERN LIGHTS

Also known as the Aurora Borealis, these are a beautiful natural phenomenon seen on Earth in the Arctic. Auroras are streams of colored light that move across the sky. These lights are caused by solar winds that are interacting with Earth's magnetic field.

NEW INTEL

Since the Sun's activity affects the weather on Earth, scientists know that learning about the Sun is important. DSCOVR, the Deep Space Climate Observatory satellite, was launched in February 2015 to monitor solar winds in real time. Its mission is to help us prevent any solar activity from interfering with GPS, power grids, or air travel on Earth.

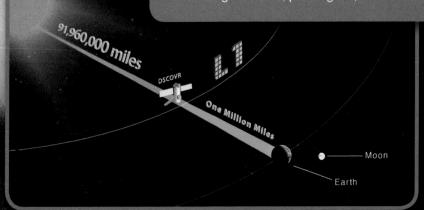

91,960,000 miles

L1

DSCOVR

One Million Miles

Moon

Earth

A rocket is a kind of engine that can travel into space. The difference between a jet engine and a rocket engine is that a jet engine needs air to work and a rocket engine doesn't. Rocket engines were designed to work without air, since there isn't any air in space.

IT *IS* ROCKET SCIENCE

Space rockets get off the ground by accelerating gases to very high speeds and then releasing them to lift off. This is similar to letting air out of a balloon—when you let the air out, the balloon takes off.

➡ A rocket is an engine, or a vehicle that holds an engine.

➡ Rockets burn fuel. Some use liquid fuel, like gasoline, and some use solid fuels, like gunpowder or coal.

➡ The rocket engine turns the fuel into gas by heating it up. As the fuel burns, the weight of the rocket decreases.

➡ The engine pushes the gas back out (the push is called thrust), which makes the rocket increase in speed (this is called acceleration).

TYPES OF ROCKETS
ROCKETS USED IN SPACE

ROCKETS USED ON EARTH

REUSABLE SPACE SHUTTLES
NASA used these to transport astronauts to and from the space station.

ION ROCKETS
An ion rocket uses electrical energy to provide thrust.

MILITARY ROCKETS
Military rockets and missile systems have been used as weapons over many years.

THREE ROCKETS THAT ROCKED THE WORLD

1. THE FIRST LIQUID-FUELED ROCKET
Dr. Robert H. Goddard was an American engineer, physicist, and inventor. On March 16, 1926, he successfully launched the first liquid-fueled rocket. The flight lasted 2.5 seconds and traveled less than a mile.

2. THE V-2
In 1942, Germany launched its first V-2 rocket. In fact, it was the first man-made object ever to enter space.

3. THE SATURN Vs
NASA (the National Aeronautics and Space Administration) launched these huge rockets 13 times from 1966 to 1973. They were used for landings on the Moon as well as for launching Skylab, the first U.S. space station.

FIREWORK ROCKETS
You've seen these on the Fourth of July. Fireworks are used for entertainment and celebrations.

SOLID FUEL ROCKETS
These rockets have motors that use solid propellants. The earliest solid-fueled rockets, which used gunpowder, were invented in China.

SATURN V OR MULTISTAGE ROCKETS
These were the largest and most powerful rockets ever built.

The Space Shuttle

"**5**... 4 ... 3 ... 2 ... 1 ... liftoff!" Space shuttles, also known as orbiters, were unique, reusable vehicles that could take people beyond Earth's atmosphere into space. A space shuttle launched with the power of a rocket, and when it returned to Earth, it landed like an airplane. NASA's space shuttle program lasted from 1981 to 2011.

GALACTIC FACT

Since 1981, there have been six space shuttle orbiters:

Enterprise
Columbia
Challenger
Discovery
Atlantis
Endeavour

RUDDER
Allowed the shuttle to turn when it was in the atmosphere.

MAIN ENGINES
Used for launch and landing.

TANK
Stored fuel.

PAYLOAD BAY
Central area that carried equipment.

REMOTE CONTROL ARM
Used to grab parts of the space station that needed repair.

FORWARD CONTROL THRUSTERS
Stabilized the altitude of the shuttle.

DELTA WINGS
Gave the spacecraft efficient speed and helped with a smooth landing.

EVELON
Flap that controlled the movement of the nose up and down. Didn't work in space.

THERMAL PROTECTION SYSTEM
Space shuttles faced harsh conditions when journeying to space and back to Earth. They traveled from the freezing temperatures of space (a frigid –250°F (–157°C)) to the heat created by friction when reentering Earth's atmosphere (a sizzling 3,000°F (1,649°C)). NASA engineers realized that sand is heat resistant. So they created sand tiles to cover the shuttle's surface like a huge puzzle. They used about 32,000 tiles per orbiter.

BY THE NUMBERS
SPACE SHUTTLES

135
SPACE SHUTTLE MISSIONS

ON A MISSION

Each time a spacecraft launched, it was called a "mission." A space shuttle could transport up to seven astronauts to the International Space Station (ISS) and carry other spacecraft, like satellites—machines that orbit the planets—and space probes, which are used to take samples of a planet's atmosphere. When NASA was building the ISS, a space shuttle carried the pieces to build it. A space shuttle also worked as a science lab, and many experiments were conducted on board.

WORKING

SLEEPING

EATING

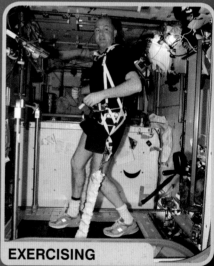

EXERCISING

USING REMOTE CONTROL ARM

MAKING REPAIRS

Before launching the first U.S. space shuttle in April 1981, NASA had many other space exploration programs. Here are a few notable early missions.

GEMINI 3

Call sign: *Molly Brown*
Mission: Maneuver while in orbit
Launch date: March 23, 1965
Duration: 4 hours, 52 minutes, 31 seconds
Crew: Gus Grissom, John Young

HIGHLIGHTS The Gemini program was the first to carry a computer for guidance and maneuvering. This technology eventually helped astronauts learn how to dock their vehicles in space.

PROJECT MERCURY 7

Call sign: *Friendship 7*
Mission: Orbit Earth
Launch date: February 20, 1962
Duration: 4 hours, 55 minutes, 23 seconds

HIGHLIGHTS John Herschel Glenn, Jr., was the third American in space. He orbited Earth three times in less than five hours.

APOLLO 11

Call sign: *Columbia, Eagle*
Mission: Land on the Moon
Launch date: July 16, 1969
Duration: 8 days, 3 hours, 18 minutes, 35 seconds
Crew: Neil Armstrong, Edwin "Buzz" Aldrin, Michael Collins

HIGHLIGHTS In addition to walking on the Moon, this crew returned with the first samples of rock and sediment from any planetary body. These samples taught scientists what the Moon was made of and how it was created.

The Moon Landing

The first person to walk on the Moon was United States astronaut Neil Armstrong, a member of the Apollo 11 mission. A camera inside the lunar module allowed for live television coverage as Armstrong climbed down to the Moon's surface. On July 20, 1969, he walked out of the spacecraft and uttered perhaps the most famous line in space exploration: "That's one small step for man, one giant leap for mankind."

APOLLO 11

Mission accomplished! Apollo 11 launched on July 16, 1969, from Cape Kennedy (now Cape Canaveral) in Florida. Four days later, the first people stepped onto the Moon's surface. On July 24, the command module splashed down in the Pacific Ocean, and a recovery ship, USS *Hornet*, picked up the astronauts.

Apollo Command Module (*Columbia*):
This was the command center for the Apollo 11 mission. It included room for three astronauts, parachutes, equipment, and engines.

Service Module:
The service module supported the command module with electricity, oxygen, and water.

Lunar Module:
This was the first manned vehicle created to operate outside of Earth's environment. The astronauts used it to get to the surface of the Moon.

Saturn V Rockets:
These heavy lift vehicles were responsible for the launch of Apollo 11. They created 7.6 million pounds (3.4 million kg) of thrust to make the launch successful.

MEN ON THE MOON

Neil Armstrong and Buzz Aldrin spent 22 hours on the Moon, while fellow astronaut Mike Collins remained in orbit. Armstrong and Aldrin collected rock and soil samples and took many photographs. An American flag was left on the Moon's surface as a reminder of this great moment in history.

Since there's no air in space, the astronauts could not take off their spacesuit hoods and speak to one another. Instead, they relied on radio equipment inside their spacesuits to talk to one another while on the Moon.

THE RACE TO THE MOON

In the 1950s and 1960s, the United States and the Soviet Union (Russia) competed to see which country had the best space technology. The competition between the two countries to put a person on the Moon would last for years.

OCTOBER 4, 1957
Soviet satellite Sputnik 1, the first man-made satellite, left Earth's atmosphere.

NOVEMBER 3, 1957
Laika the dog traveled to space, sent by the Soviets in Sputnik 2.

APRIL 12, 1961
Soviet cosmonaut Yury Gagarin was the first man to orbit Earth.

MAY 5, 1961:
Alan Shepard was the first American in space.

MAY 25, 1961
President John F. Kennedy told Congress that he wanted the United States to be the first to put a man on the Moon and return him safely to Earth.

FEBRUARY 20, 1962
American John Glenn launched *Friendship 7* and orbited Earth.

JUNE 16, 1963
Soviet Valentina Tereshkova was the first woman in space.

MARCH 18, 1965
Soviet Aleksey Arkhipovich Leonov took the first walk in space.

JULY 20, 1969
The United States won the race to the Moon.

Becoming an Astronaut

An astronaut is a person trained to be a pilot on a spacecraft and travel and work in space. Astronauts are trained at NASA. Training centers in the United States are located at the Johnson Space Center in Texas, and the Kennedy Space Center in Florida.

DO YOU WANT TO BE AN ASTRONAUT?

Here are some things to consider:

➡ It takes many years of studying. You need to go to college and have a master's degree or even a PhD.

➡ You need to study engineering, medicine, or one of the sciences. Many astronauts are also military pilots.

➡ You need to speak English and even Russian or Japanese, so you can talk to astronauts from other countries.

➡ You must be very healthy, since astronaut training is extremely hard.

➡ You need to be able to work well with others. Astronauts work in small spaces, so you have to be able to be courteous and friendly.

ASTRONAUTS IN TRAINING

Astronauts do not just hop on a spacecraft and fly. They need training. They have to be in excellent physical condition, and they need to train on simulators and underwater to get used to life in weightless (also known as zero-g) conditions. Astronauts use a special multi-axis trainer (MAT) to get used to the spinning they will experience when they are weightless and disoriented. They also need to prepare for space walks and learn how to balance themselves.

MULTI-AXIS TRAINER

ZERO-G CONDITIONS

THE VOMIT COMET

One of the most talked-about astronaut training centers is NASA's "Vomit Comet." This simulator introduces astronauts in training to the feeling of weightlessness in space. The astronauts climb aboard, and the aircraft moves in a trajectory that creates weightlessness for 25 seconds. Unfortunately, this makes the astronauts feel sick to their stomachs until they get used to it.

THE VOMIT COMET

AT A GLANCE

HOW THE SOLAR SYSTEM WORKS

➡ Gravity, spin, and balance

➡ How planets are born

THE INNER SOLAR SYSTEM

➡ The Terrestrial (or Earth-like)
  Planets include:

  • Mercury, the smallest
    and fastest-spinning

  • Venus, the hottest

  • Earth, the only habitable planet

  • Mars, with an iron-rich surface

THE OUTER SOLAR SYSTEM

➡ The Jovian (or Gaseous)
  Planets include:

  • Saturn, ringed, made of rock and ice

  • Jupiter, with 67 moons

  • Uranus, the coldest planet

  • Neptune, with the strongest winds

THE KUIPER BELT

➡ A zone of icy objects in
  the outer solar system

➡ Includes Pluto and other
  dwarf planets

THE INTERNATIONAL
SPACE STATION

➡ Orbits Earth

➡ Where astronauts live
  and study space

The Milky Way

The Solar System

The Solar System formed 4.6 billion years ago from a large cloud of dust and gas. The Solar System includes the Sun and all the families of celestial objects that orbit around it. It includes eight planets and their moons, the Asteroid Belt, the Kuiper Belt (a distant region of icy dwarf planets and many other objects), and the Oort Cloud, another faraway place with trillions of icy objects, where it is thought our comets originated. We'll take a look at how we explore our Solar System, including what it's like to live in space at the International Space Station.

Perfect Harmony

All the planets in our Solar System revolve around the Sun. But why? There are several factors at work. Each object orbits the center of mass for its system, and for our Solar System that center is the Sun. Each planet is at the perfect distance and moving at the right speed to maintain its own orbit—it has momentum. And no matter how big or small an object is, there is a curvature of space at work as well. In short, the planets and the Sun are in perfect balance. Let's look at some of the forces at work here.

Mercury
Venus
Earth
Mars
Asteroid Belt
Jupiter
Saturn
Uranus
Neptune
Kuiper Belt

IT'S ALL ABOUT THE CURVE

When scientists talk about spacetime, they are talking about a mathematical combination of space and time. It would take an entire book to cover this complex topic, but there is a simple way to think about it in understanding gravity and how our solar system works. As objects speed through space, seemingly in a straight line, through the combined effect of space and time they follow a curved path. It is the combination of this curve, and gravity, that holds objects in their orbit.

Oort Cloud

PLANETS

The farther away a planet is from the Sun, the longer it takes to orbit the Sun. The longer the orbit, the longer the planet's year is. It takes Mercury about three Earth months and Neptune more than 164 Earth years to orbit the Sun.

GRAVITATIONAL PULL

Everything with mass or energy has a gravitational pull. The Sun has great gravitational force and has the power to pull all the planets towards it. So why don't the planets crash into the Sun and burn?

ORBITAL MOTION
This kind of momentum is what prevents the planets from being pulled into the Sun. While the Sun's gravity pulls them toward the Sun, their rotation is pushing them outward toward empty space. So the planets maintain their distance from the Sun.

ANGULAR MOMENTUM
Things in rotation have momentum, which means they keep doing what they are doing. This is called angular momentum. Earth rotates on its axis, and it keeps rotating because of this momentum. This kind of momentum means that things in rotation don't change direction.

BY THE NUMBERS
EARTH DAYS TO ORBIT THE SUN

88
EARTH DAYS ON MERCURY
0.24 Earth Years

224.7
EARTH DAYS ON VENUS
0.62 Earth Years

365.25
EARTH DAYS ON EARTH
1.00 Earth Years

687
EARTH DAYS ON MARS
1.88 Earth Years

4,322.6
EARTH DAYS ON JUPITER
11.86 Earth Years

10,759.2
EARTH DAYS ON SATURN
29.46 Earth Years

30,685.4
EARTH DAYS ON URANUS
84.07 Earth Years

60,189
EARTH DAYS ON NEPTUNE
164.81 Earth Years

Astronomical discoveries have been made since ancient times. In the 2nd millennium BC, the Babylonians discovered Mercury, Venus, Mars, Jupiter, and Saturn. However, those would remain the only identified planets until the invention of the telescope. It wasn't until the scientific revolution in 1514 that astronomy really took off.

Halley's Comet in motion

TO INFINITY AND BEYOND!
A TIMELINE OF SOLAR SYSTEM DISCOVERIES

1514
Nicolaus Copernicus, an astronomer and mathematician, presented his theory that the Earth revolves around the Sun.

1609 ▶
Johannes Kepler presented two laws of planetary motion. He presented his third law ten years later.

Johannes Kepler

1757 ▶
Astronomer and geophysicist Edmond Halley predicted the orbit of the comet later named for him.

1915
Proxima Centauri, our closest star after the Sun, was discovered by Scottish astronomer Robert Innes.

Edmond Halley

NASA has honored Kepler by naming a mission after him, the Kepler Mission, tasked with finding other Earth-like planets. Here is the Discovery Mission #10 under construction.

STAR SCIENTIST

JOHANNES KEPLER

(1571-1630)

Johannes Kepler was a mathematician and astronomer. He is remembered most for his Three Laws of Planetary Motion.

1. THE LAW OF ELLIPSES

Each planet moves around the Sun in an elliptical shape. Previously, people thought the Sun orbited Earth and that planets moved in circles.

2. THE LAW OF EQUAL AREAS

Planets move faster when they are closer to the Sun. This replaced the idea that planets all moved at the same speed.

3. THE LAW OF HARMONIES

If we know the amount of time it takes for a planet to travel around the Sun, we can figure out that planet's distance from the Sun. The opposite applies, as well.

This work helped Isaac Newton later create his theory of gravity. Kepler was also the founder of modern optics: He discovered eyeglasses for nearsightedness and farsightedness.

1950

Jan Oort discovered a mass of comets that orbit the sun, later named the Oort Cloud.

1973 ▶

Pioneer 10 was the first spacecraft to pass through the Asteroid Belt on its way toward Jupiter, Saturn, and the Milky Way.

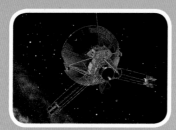

Spacecraft Pioneer 10 in orbit

1979 ▶

Saturn and its rings were photographed for the first time.

1995

The Hubble Space Telescope took one of the most famous photographs in history: the Eagle Nebula, which astronomers call the "Pillars of Creation."

Saturn's rings

Birth of a Planet

The Inner Solar System is home to four terrestrial planets: Mercury, Venus, Earth, and Mars. Mercury is the smallest, Venus is the hottest, Earth is only planet that has surface liquid H2O (water), and Mars has most varied terrain.

The Jovian planets are the big guys! The largest four planets are in the Outer Solar System: Jupiter, Saturn, Uranus, and Neptune. The word "Jovian" comes from the word "Jupiter," also known as "Jove." Even though they are nicknamed the Gas Giants, they are not made entirely of gas.

HOW PLANETS FORM

Where did the planets come from? A planet is formed from the dust remnants of a supernova. The dust forms into disks around young stars. At the center of the disk is a protostar. Surrounding the young star is a nebular disk. The materials within this disk collide with one another and accrete—grow together adding layers slowly—to form larger planets.

THE GAS/DUST CLOUD ROTATES

The motion inside the cloud makes it churn, and everything is mixed together. After it churns, the cloud begins to rotate.

THE CLOUD FLATTENS

The rotating cloud flattens into a disk. These disks are the birthplaces of all planets and stars.

THE MATERIAL CLUMPS

As the disk spins, bigger pieces—which move more quickly than smaller pieces because they experience less wind resistance—sweep up the smaller pieces. In this way, baby planets get bigger through accretion. Scientists call these forming planets *planetesimals*.

THE PLANETESIMAL GROWS

Hundreds of planetesimals form within the cloud at the same time. They grab pieces of material in their path, such as slow-moving space rocks and gas. Sometimes they smash into each other. Sometimes gravity draws them together. Other times they merge with another object to create a planet.

Sequence of planetary formation, from top to bottom.

NEW INTEL

It's snowing in space! Astronomers have found a snow area in what they believe is a baby solar system about 175 light-years away. The snow is made of carbon dioxide, not water. They named this snow line "TW Hydrae."

TERRESTRIAL PLANETS

➡ Majority of planet is rock.

➡ Have a molten heavy metal core.

➡ Are closer to the Sun.

➡ May or may not have a moon.

➡ Lost the hydrogen and helium they originally had.

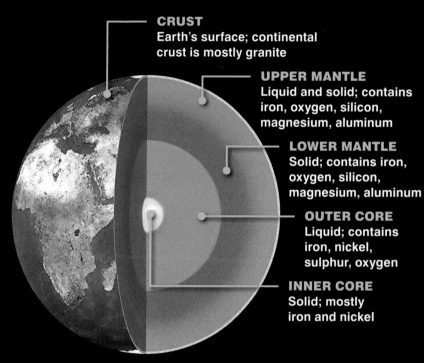

CRUST
Earth's surface; continental crust is mostly granite

UPPER MANTLE
Liquid and solid; contains iron, oxygen, silicon, magnesium, aluminum

LOWER MANTLE
Solid; contains iron, oxygen, silicon, magnesium, aluminum

OUTER CORE
Liquid; contains iron, nickel, sulphur, oxygen

INNER CORE
Solid; mostly iron and nickel

Terrestrial planet structure: Earth

JOVIAN PLANETS

➡ Majority of planet is gas.

➡ Have rocky cores.

➡ Are farther from the Sun.

➡ Have many moons and rings.

➡ Contain hydrogen and helium.

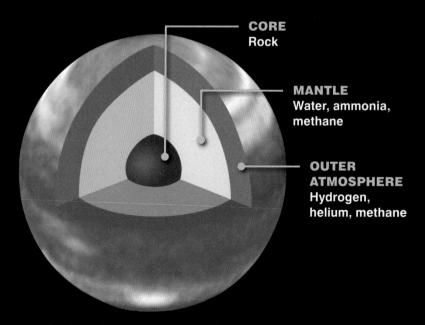

CORE
Rock

MANTLE
Water, ammonia, methane

OUTER ATMOSPHERE
Hydrogen, helium, methane

Jovian planet structure: Neptune

STELLAR STATS
MERCURY

NAME
➡ Mercury, named after the mythological messenger of the Roman gods

NICKNAME
➡ The Swift Planet

DIAMETER
➡ 3,032 miles (4,080 km)

MASS
➡ 5.5% of Earth's mass

GRAVITY COMPARED TO EARTH
➡ 0.38

DISTANCE FROM EARTH
➡ 47 million miles (76 million km)

DISTANCE FROM SUN
➡ 36 million miles (58 million km)

LENGTH OF YEAR
➡ 88 Earth days

LENGTH OF DAY
➡ 176 Earth days

AVERAGE TEMPERATURE
➡ 333°F (167°C)

SURFACE DETAILS
➡ Impact craters

NUMBER OF MOONS
➡ 0

Mercury faces the Sun, so temperatures sizzle! Did you know this planet is hot enough to melt lead? After Venus, Mercury is the hottest planet in the entire solar system. Scientists believe Mercury got knocked around a lot when the solar system first formed. The evidence is on the surface—tons of craters. In fact, with all of its holes, wrinkles, and bumps, Mercury looks very much like our Moon.

THAT'S ASTRONOMICAL!

Crater in Caloris Basin

Mercury's Caloris Basin crater is 960 miles (1,545 km) wide and 1.25 miles (2 km) deep, formed when a space rock crashed into the planet billions of years ago. The crater is so big that it would take more than 16 hours to drive from one end of the crater to the other, going at highway speed.

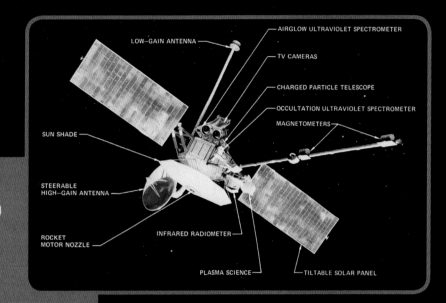

LOW–GAIN ANTENNA
AIRGLOW ULTRAVIOLET SPECTROMETER
TV CAMERAS
CHARGED PARTICLE TELESCOPE
OCCULTATION ULTRAVIOLET SPECTROMETER
MAGNETOMETERS
SUN SHADE
STEERABLE HIGH–GAIN ANTENNA
ROCKET MOTOR NOZZLE
INFRARED RADIOMETER
PLASMA SCIENCE
TILTABLE SOLAR PANEL

MERCURY: MARINER 10

MISSION STARTED
November 3, 1973

MISSION ENDED
March 24, 1975

GOAL
To study Mercury. The Mariner 10 was able to photograph the surface of Mercury and measure its temperature.

RESULT
During this time it mapped just under half of the planet's surface. Astronauts also discovered that Mercury had even more wrinkled ridges and eventually concluded that Mercury shrunk about 4 miles (6.4 km) in radius in the time between the Messenger and Mariner missions (1973-2004).

GALACTIC FACT

Mercury is our smallest and fastest-orbiting planet. It zooms around the Sun at 105,947 miles per hour (170,505 kph).

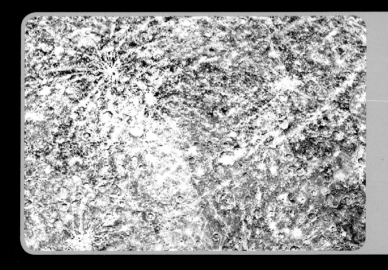

MERCURY HAS WRINKLES

Mercury got too much Sun! As the planet's molten iron core started to cool, it contracted, which created wrinkles on the surface. Scientists named the wrinkles "Lobate Scarps." These wrinkles can be up to a mile high and hundreds of miles or kilometers long. They look just like the mountain ranges we have on Earth.

STELLAR STATS
VENUS

NAME
➡ Venus, named for the Roman goddess of love and beauty

NICKNAME
➡ The Evening Star

DIAMETER
➡ 7,522 miles (12,105 km)

MASS
➡ 81.5% of Earth's mass

GRAVITY COMPARED TO EARTH
➡ 0.91

DISTANCE FROM EARTH
➡ 25 million miles (40 million km)

DISTANCE FROM SUN
➡ 67 million miles (108 million km)

LENGTH OF YEAR
➡ 224.7 Earth days

LENGTH OF DAY
➡ 117 Earth days

AVERAGE TEMPERATURE
➡ 867°F (464°C)

SURFACE DETAILS
➡ Volcanoes, maybe active, impact craters

NUMBER OF MOONS
➡ 0

There are 1,000 volcanoes on Venus. To get to its volcanic surface, you'd have to make it through poisonous gases, hurricane-force winds, and lightning. Venus has thick clouds made of carbon dioxide and sulfuric acid. These gases reflect the Sun's light and make Venus shine very brightly. After the Sun and Moon, Venus is the brightest object in our sky. It has two nicknames, the Morning Star and the Evening Star, because it can be seen at sunrise and just after sunset.

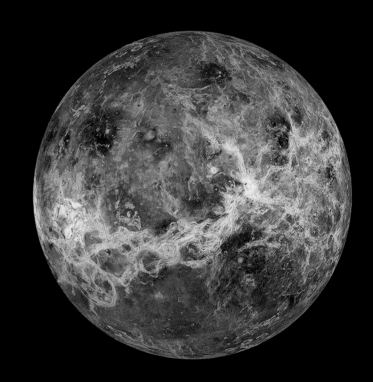

GALACTIC FACT

Venus rotates on its axis in the opposite direction than other planets. Unlike on Earth, on Venus the sun rises in the west and sets in the east.

MAAT MONS

Just below the acid clouds are dome-shaped volcanoes. The largest, Maat Mons, is five miles high and about the size of the Big Island in Hawaii. In 1991, the Magellan spacecraft took photos and observed fresh lava.

EARTH'S "TWIN"

Venus is often called Earth's "twin sister" because they are of similar size and weight. But they are different in important ways. Venus's atmosphere is toxic and over 100 times thicker than Earth's, and Venus has no water.

Pioneer Venus Orbiter being built

PIONEER VENUS MISSION

MISSION STARTED
August 8, 1978

MISSION ENDED
October 8, 1992

GOAL
Investigate the winds on Venus.

RESULT
Probes were sent down to Venus from the spacecraft and sent data to Earth. The data let scientists know the different temperatures on Venus and what the atmosphere was made of.

U nlike the other planets in our solar system, conditions on Earth are nicely balanced to support life. Earth has an atmosphere that protects us from the Sun but also keeps us warm. Water on Earth is plentiful in the forms of solid (ice), liquid (water), and gas (clouds).

STELLAR STATS
EARTH

NAME
➡ Earth, from the German word "erde," meaning "ground"

NICKNAME
➡ The Blue Planet

DIAMETER
➡ 7,926 miles (12,756 km)

MASS
➡ 13.2 septillion pounds (5.9 sextillion kg)

GRAVITY COMPARED TO EARTH
➡ 1.0

DISTANCE FROM SUN
➡ 92,960,000 miles (147 million km)

LENGTH OF YEAR
➡ 365.25 days

LENGTH OF DAY
➡ 24 hours

AVERAGE TEMPERATURE
➡ 59°F (15°C)

SURFACE DETAILS
➡ Rocky, oceans, polar ice

NUMBER OF MOONS
➡ 1

WHAT'S IN A NAME?

Earth is the only planet in the Solar System not named after a mythical god. Earth has had its name for at least 1,000 years but there is no record of exactly who named it. If you discovered a new planet, what would you name it?

EARTH'S ROTATION IS SLOWING DOWN

Earth's spin is slowing by 17 milliseconds every hundred years. This will eventually create longer days on Earth. But don't worry, it's not expected to happen for another 140 million years!

IT'S NOT PERFECT

Earth isn't a perfectly round sphere; it's actually shaped like an orange. It's fat in the middle and smaller at both the North Pole and South Pole. The diameter at the Equator measures 7,926 miles (12,756 km), and at each pole, it's 7,891 miles (12,699 km).

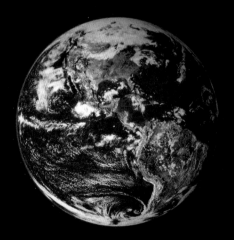

Earth

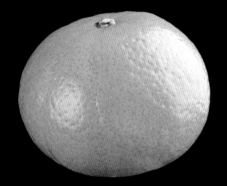

Orange

BY THE NUMBERS
EARTH

5.5
MILES (8.9 km)
Tallest peak,
Mount Everest

6.8
MILES (11 km)
Deepest ocean depth,
the Mariana Trench

3,000
MILES (4,828 km)
Largest desert, the
Sahara Desert

Earth's Anatomy

The entire Earth is made of rocks and minerals. Inside planet Earth there is a liquid core of molten rock and on the outside there is a hard crust. Earth's crust is covered by soil, water, sand and ice. Scientists called geologists study the rocks and soil on the surface of Earth's land and oceans. They drill holes in the rocks to learn more about them, how old they are, and what they are made of.

WORD

Mass is the amount of matter in an object. It's based on the total number of atoms, the density of the atoms, and the type of atoms in an object. Weight is a result of gravity, but the mass of an object remains constant.

LAYERS OF THE EARTH

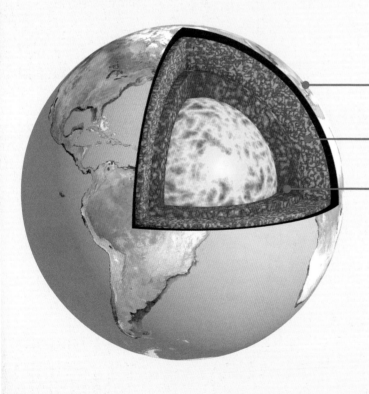

1. CRUST
Earth's crust is like a shell. It's 20 to 30 miles (32 to 48 km) thick, and is thicker—up to 43 miles (69 km) thick—in places with mountains. Made of oxygen, magnesium, aluminum, silicon, calcium, sodium, potassium, and iron, it makes up only 1% of Earth's mass.

2. MANTLE
The Earth's mantle is molten rock and makes up 70% of Earth's mass. This is the largest part. It is made up of oxygen, silicon, aluminum and iron.

3. OUTER CORE AND INNER CORE
The core of Earth is made up of iron and nickel. It holds about 30% of Earth's mass. The outer core is liquid iron and nickel and the inner core is solid iron and nickel.

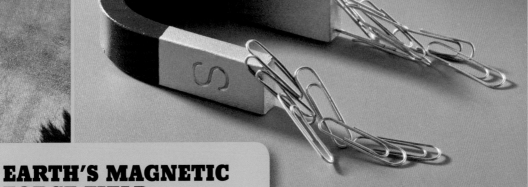

EARTH'S MAGNETIC FORCE FIELD

Earth has a magnetic field. Its core is made of molten (liquified) metal. As Earth rotates, the iron moves around. This creates a magnetic field that actually extends 37,000 miles (60,000 km) into space. Called the magnetosphere, this force field protects Earth from solar winds and cosmic rays.

ASK HAKEEM...

WHY DOES A COMPASS ALWAYS POINT NORTH?

You'll never get lost with a compass in hand. That's because a compass has a small magnetic pin suspended in it that can spin, causing it to react to Earth's magnetism. A compass points north because all magnets have two poles, north and south. The north end of a compass magnet is drawn to align with Earth's magnetic field.

WORD

Weight is the measure of the force of gravity on an object. The weight of an object can change based on location. This is why your weight would be different on other planets.

Earth's Atmosphere

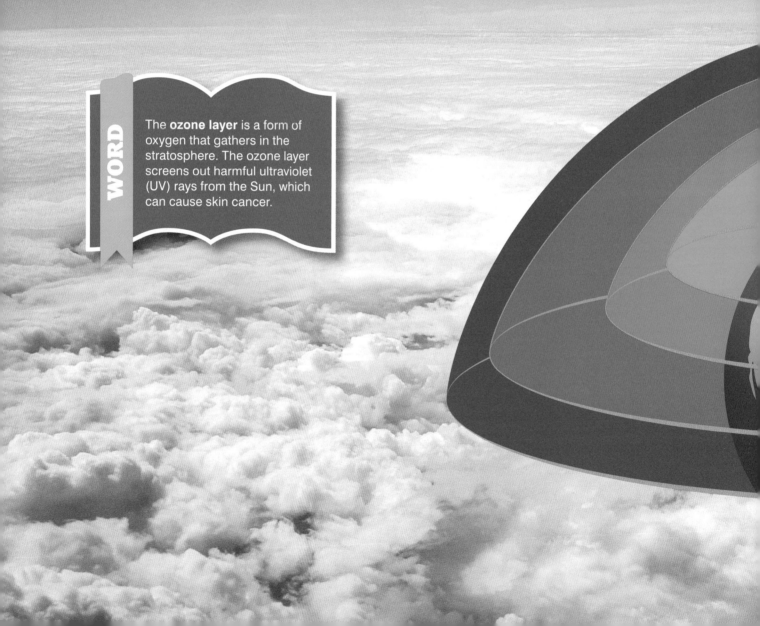

The Earth is cradled in a layer of gases called the atmosphere. This atmosphere provides protection, shielding us from excess rays of the Sun while also absorbing some sunlight for warmth. The atmosphere holds in the heat and keeps the temperature balanced. In most places, it's never too hot during the day or too cold at night for us to survive.

Earth's atmosphere is made of nitrogen, oxygen, water vapor, carbon dioxide, and other gases. It's held in place by Earth's gravity so it cannot dissolve into space. The gases in the atmosphere are thicker and denser closest to the surface of Earth. The higher up you travel in our sky, the thinner the atmosphere becomes.

WORD

The **ozone layer** is a form of oxygen that gathers in the stratosphere. The ozone layer screens out harmful ultraviolet (UV) rays from the Sun, which can cause skin cancer.

LAYERS OF THE ATMOSPHERE

THERMOSPHERE
Includes both the exosphere and the ionosphere, and is the largest of all the layers. This is where space shuttles and satellites orbit.

EXOSPHERE
400-800 miles (644-1,288 km) from Earth's surface. The outermost layer, where the air is very thin, and the environment is similar to space.

IONOSPHERE
50-400 miles (80-644 km) from Earth's surface. This is where auroras happen, like the Aurora Borealis.

MESOPAUSE

MESOSPHERE
30-50 miles (48-80 km) from Earth's surface. Where meteors burn up and disappear. The fast-travelling meteor gets so hot when it hits the mesosphere, it glows.

STRATOPAUSE

STRATOSPHERE
10-30 miles (16-48 km) from Earth's surface. Planes fly here. Ozone increases, and temperatures rise, higher in the stratosphere.

TROPOPAUSE

TROPOSPHERE
0-10 miles (0-16 km) from Earth's surface. This is the atmosphere we are surrounded by every day. At the top of the troposphere, the air is cooler. The bottom is warmer, because the ground holds in heat.

STELLAR STATS
MARS

NAME
➡ Mars, named for the Roman God of War

NICKNAME
➡ The Red Planet

DIAMETER
➡ 4,220 miles (6,791 km)

MASS
➡ 10.7% of Earth's mass

GRAVITY COMPARED TO EARTH
➡ 0.38

DISTANCE FROM EARTH
➡ 140 million miles (225 million km)

DISTANCE FROM SUN
➡ 141.6 million miles (228 million km)

LENGTH OF YEAR
➡ 687 Earth days

LENGTH OF DAY
➡ 24 Earth hours, 43 minutes

AVERAGE TEMPERATURE
➡ -80°F (-62°C)

SURFACE DETAILS
➡ Rocky with ancient volcanoes, impact craters

NUMBER OF MOONS
➡ 2

The planet most like Earth is Mars. A day on Mars is about the same length as ours. There are winds, sandy deserts, and seasons. But it differs from Earth in important ways. It's incredibly cold and the atmosphere is too thin for people to survive without a spacesuit. Scientists believe there may be water on Mars, and plan to continue using robots called rovers to uncover the planet's history.

GALACTIC FACT

Mars' path around the Sun is more oval-shaped than that of other planets. This means the seasons on Mars last longer—in fact, twice as long as on Earth. Mars and Earth are the only planets that have seaons.

Moon

Mars

Saturn

Mars can be seen in the night sky without a telescope.

MOUNTAINS

The tallest mountain in the entire solar system is located on Mars. Named Olympus Mons, it measures 16 miles (26 km) high and 374 miles (602 km) wide. Olympus Mons is as wide as the entire state of Arizona and is three times higher than Earth's Mount Everest.

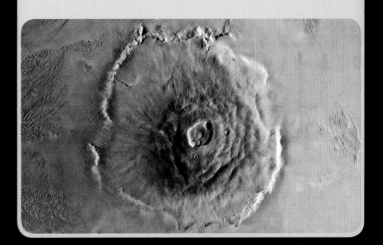

TWO MOONS

In 1877, scientist Asaph Hall discovered that Mars has two small moons. Almost a century later, NASA's Mariner 9 spacecraft became the first man-made satellite to orbit another planet. Images from the mission revealed that both moons, named Phobos and Deimos, have "lumpy" shapes rather than round.

Deimos

Phobos

Is There Water on Mars?

Mars is a very chilly planet. Scientists believe Mars used to have a thicker atmosphere, was warmer than it is now, and had water on its surface.

THE EVIDENCE OF WATER

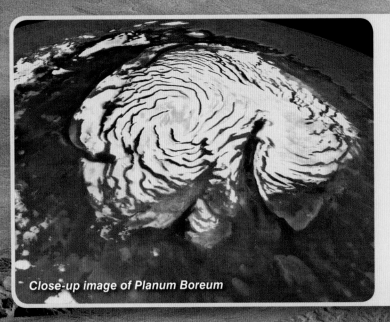

Close-up image of Planum Boreum

ICE CAPS

Mars is the only other planet besides Earth that has polar ice caps. The ice caps on Mars are made of dry ice (frozen carbon dioxide), which means they're much colder than ice on earth. The northern cap is called Planum Boreum. The southern ice cap is called the Planum Australe. Scientists think there may be liquid water beneath the frozen ice caps.

ATMOSPHERE

Mars' atmosphere is 95% carbon dioxide with some nitrogen, oxygen, and argon, and is very thin. Scientists think it used to be thicker and various things could have happened to it. One theory is that it floated away into space and was destroyed by solar winds. The gravity on Mars is weak, so it cannot hold its atmosphere in place.

Martian atmosphere (shown as purple in this image)

GALACTIC FACT

Scientists think it hasn't rained on Mars in 3 billion years.

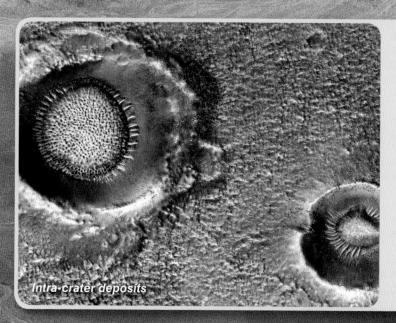

Intra-crater deposits

CRATERS

Winding channels, rocky paths, and large craters suggest there used to be large amounts of running water on Mars. This could have been melting ice or rain or even snow. Some scientists believe there was a large ocean on Mars.

DELTA

The Aeolis Dorsa is a huge plain, about 620 miles wide. Scientists are investigating a river delta leading to a large area that could be the bottom of an ancient ocean on Mars.

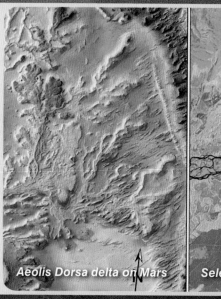

Aeolis Dorsa delta on Mars

Selenga delta on Earth

After Earth, Mars is the planet that could become the most hospitable to life as we know it. This makes it an exciting place to explore. NASA has used rovers to journey to Mars to investigate and take photographs. Their findings have uncovered some amazing new information. But before the rovers could make the trip, scientists needed to figure out how to make them.

MARS ROVERS

Rovers are robots with wheels to drive over the planet's surface. Some rover designs were inspired by animals, to move over any kind of terrain. They are outfitted with cameras used in navigation and in image data collection, spectrometers to measure wavelengths, energy, and light, radiation detectors, environmental and atmospheric sensors.

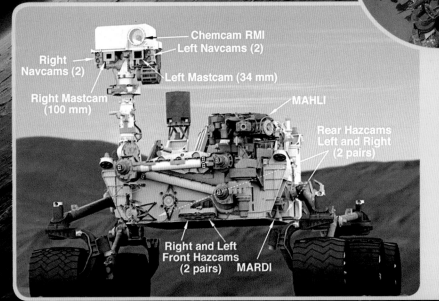

Chemcam RMI
Left Navcams (2)
Right Navcams (2)
Left Mastcam (34 mm)
Right Mastcam (100 mm)
MAHLI
Rear Hazcams Left and Right (2 pairs)
Right and Left Front Hazcams (2 pairs)   MARDI

MISSION: CURIOSITY

LAUNCHED
November 26, 2011

STATUS
Ongoing

Curiosity's mission is to explore the soil and rocks to find out what the planet's environment was like in the past. Here is a look at the rover and its observational tools.

MISSION: MARS EXPLORATION ROVER (MER)
SPIRIT AND OPPORTUNITY

OPPORTUNITY

LAUNCHED
July 7, 2003

STATUS
Ongoing

SPIRIT

LAUNCHED
June 10, 2003

STATUS
Last transmission March 22, 2010

These rovers arrived on Mars in January 2004 to search for signs of ancient water activity. They were only supposed to last three months. Spirit stopped communicating in March 2010. As of 2015, Opportunity is still roving. Spirit discovered volcanic rock, which suggests there were volcanic explosions on Mars that included magma and water. Opportunity found a very large rock made of nickel and iron, which was the very first meteorite ever discovered on another planet.

Panoramic photo of Mars taken by Opportunity.

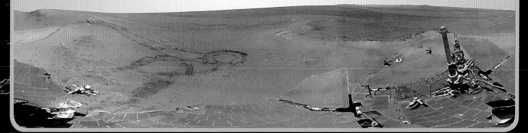

MISSION: PATHFINDER

LAUNCHED
December 4, 1996

STATUS
Last data transmission on September 27, 1997

This mission was created so scientists could deliver a robotic rover to Mars to investigate the surface. The wagon-like rover Sojourner entered Mars' atmosphere by parachute. It took samples of rocks and more than 500 images. This hardworking rover returned a huge amount of data for scientists to study.

A year-long worldwide essay competition led to the naming of Sojourner. Students were asked to choose a heroine and explain how his or her accomplishments fit the Pathfinder mission, and the winning essay proposed Sojourner Truth, a 19th century abolitionist and women's right activist.

STELLAR STATS
JUPITER

NAME
➡ Jupiter, named for the king of the gods in Roman mythology

NICKNAME
➡ The Giant Planet

DIAMETER
➡ 88,700 miles (142,700 km)

MASS
➡ 317 times Earth's mass

GRAVITY COMPARED TO EARTH
➡ 2.36

DISTANCE FROM EARTH
➡ 365 million miles (587 million km)

DISTANCE FROM SUN
➡ 483,800,000 miles (779 million km)

LENGTH OF YEAR
➡ 11.86 Earth years

LENGTH OF DAY
➡ 9 Earth hours, 56 minutes

AVERAGE TEMPERATURE
➡ -166°F (-110°C)

SURFACE DETAILS
➡ No solid surface

NUMBER OF MOONS
➡ 67

Jupiter is the king of the planets for many reasons. It is the largest planet in the solar system, the fastest-spinning planet, and it has more moons than any other planet. And it is recognized for its Great Red Spot, a giant storm that has lasted almost 400 years!

Jupiter is made of the same elements as stars. Its atmosphere is made up of mostly hydrogen and helium (just like our Sun). Jupiter's surface is covered in thick brown, white, red, and yellow clouds. These clouds are poisonous, and the quick spinning of the planet makes Jupiter look striped.

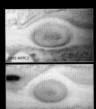

1995 WFPC2

2008 WFC3/UVIS

2014 WFC3/UVIS

THE STORMS OF JUPITER

Jupiter is known for its Great Red Spot. But it's not really a spot, it's a storm that comes from inside the planet. The Great Red Spot is similar to the hurricanes we have on Earth, but bigger. How big? Scientists estimate this storm is twice the size of Earth. Winds inside this hurricane top out at 425 miles per hour (684 kph). The storms tend to be a rusty, red color but scientists don't know why.

THAT'S ASTRONOMICAL!

Jupiter is so big you could fit 1,300 Earths inside it.

JUPITER'S RINGS

In 1979, Voyager 1 took a single photo of a faint ring around Jupiter. Voyager 2 visited the planet a few months later and helped scientists discover there were three parts to the ring.

Jupiter has 67 moons. Its four largest moons are called the Galilean Moons after Italian astronomer Galileo Galilei, who discovered them in 1610. The discovery of the Galilean Moons orbiting Jupiter helped scientists at the time realize the planets revolved around the Sun and not Earth.

GALILEAN MOONS

Ganymede is the largest moon in the solar system. Its diameter is 3,273 miles (5,268 km)—that's larger than the planet Mercury. Ganymede's atmosphere has oxygen, but not enough to support life.

Callisto is also a record-setter. It's the third largest moon in the solar system, it's one of the oldest objects, and it has the most craters.

Io is Jupiter's most volcanically active moon and is the driest object in the solar system. Its volcanic ash is sent 190 miles (396 km) above the surface.

The smallest of Jupiter's four largest moons, Europa has an icy surface. Scientists believe there is a rocky surface similar to Earth's under the ice layer. There is evidence of salty oceans on Europa, but no evidence that life has ever existed on this moon.

STAR SCIENTIST

GALILEO GALILEI

(1564-1642)

Galileo Galilei was an Italian physicist, engineer, mathematician, astronomer, and philosopher. He was not first to invent the telescope, but he created his own version with several lenses that, when used together, made a greater magnification of 30x.

Galileo used his telescope to learn more about space. He observed the Sun and was the first to discover patches on the Sun we now know are sunspots. Galileo was the first astronomer to see craters, mountains, and valleys on the Moon, and he discovered the four moons of Jupiter: Io, Ganymede, Europa and Callisto.

BY THE NUMBERS

LARGEST MOONS IN THE SOLAR SYSTEM (DIAMETER)

3,273
MILES (5,268 km)
Ganymede – Jupiter

3,201
MILES (5,152 km)
Titan – Saturn

2,985
MILES (4,805 km)
Callisto – Jupiter

2,159
MILES (3,475 km)
Earth's Moon

1,942
MILES (3,125 km)
Io – Jupiter

1,900
MILES (3,058 km)
Europa – Jupiter

1,680
MILES (2,700 km)
Triton – Neptune

1,000
MILES (1,609 km)
Titania – Uranus

Saturn is one cool planet. It has a surface temperature of -288°F (-178°C). As cold as it is on its surface, its core temperature is superhot, reaching 21,000°F (11,650°C). How can that be? Saturn's core was formed during the early solar system years and had a rocky middle. Scientists believe the rock trapped hot gases in the core.

STELLAR STATS
SATURN

NAME
➡ Saturn, named for the Roman god of agriculture, Saturnus

DIAMETER
➡ 73,367 miles (118,073 km)

MASS
➡ 95 times Earth's mass

GRAVITY COMPARED TO EARTH
➡ 0.92

KNOWN RINGS
➡ 30 (7 sets)

DISTANCE FROM EARTH
➡ 746 million miles (1.2 billion km)

DISTANCE FROM SUN
➡ 885,904,700 miles (1.4 billion km)

LENGTH OF YEAR
➡ 29.46 Earth years

LENGTH OF DAY
➡ 10 Earth hours, 40 minutes

AVERAGE TEMPERATURE
➡ -220°F (-140°C)

SURFACE DETAILS
➡ No solid surface

NUMBER OF MOONS
➡ 62

GALACTIC FACT

Saturn is the flattest planet in our solar system. It's light and spins fast. It takes Saturn less than 11 hours to make a full rotation. The faster it spins, the flatter it gets.

SMALL MOONS

The small moons are chunky blocks of ice that are smaller than 190 miles (306 km) wide.

MEDIUM MOONS

These measure 250 to 1,000 miles across (402-1,609 km). Astronomers believe these moons formed around the same time Saturn did.

LARGE MOONS

Titan, Saturn's biggest moon, is 3,220 miles across (5,182 km), which is about the diameter of the United States. Titan has liquid methane lakes and seas, making it the only other place in the Solar System than Earth that has liquid on the surface.

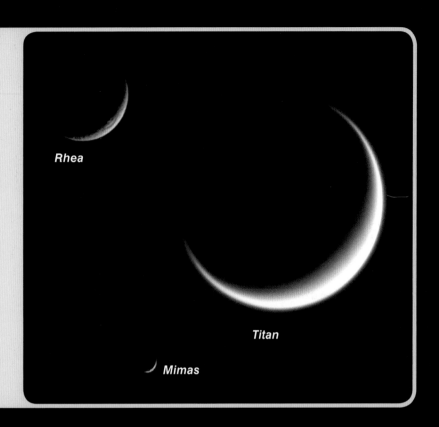

Rhea

Titan

Mimas

NEW INTEL

Using the Hubble Space Telescope, scientists discovered that there are auroras on Saturn. Like the Aurora Borealis on Earth, there are beautiful light shows on both poles of Saturn.

Saturn's Rings

Saturn's rings are made of billions of pieces of ice, rocks and space dust. Some particles are as small as a grain of sand while other particles are as large as a car. These pieces come together and look like a ring. The shiniest, most brilliant pieces of ice are newer. Astronomers know this because the sparkling pieces of ice haven't collected any dust.

The large chunks within the rings are thought to be pieces of comets or asteroids. It's a possibility that the rings are also made up of moons that were destroyed by tidal forces from Saturn's gravity.

THAT'S ASTRONOMICAL!

Saturn's rings are 169,800 miles wide (273,270 km) but less than a mile thick (less than 2 km).

DISCOVERING THE RINGS

Galileo Galilei was the first to see Saturn's rings in 1610, but he didn't have a powerful enough telescope to recognize them as rings. He thought they were handles or arms. In 1659, aided by a more powerful telescope, Dutch astronomer Christiaan Huygens identified them as actual rings.

Christiaan Huygens

HOW ARE SATURN'S RINGS FORMED?

Scientists believe Saturn has had rings since the early formation of the Solar System and they think that Saturn's rings recycle themselves. Astronomers studying the E ring on Saturn noticed that the ice geysers on Saturn's moon, Enceladus, erupt and send ice particles to the E ring.

BY THE NUMBERS
SATURN

30
RINGS

7
SETS OF RINGS
Letter-named
from A to G

STELLAR STATS
URANUS

NAME
➡ Uranus is the only planet named after a Greek God, rather than a Roman one.

NICKNAME
➡ The Ice Planet

DIAMETER
➡ 31,763 miles (51,118 km)

MASS
➡ 14.5 times Earth's mass

GRAVITY COMPARED TO EARTH
➡ 0.89

NUMBER OF RINGS
➡ 13

DISTANCE FROM EARTH
➡ 1.6 billion miles (2.6 billion km)

DISTANCE FROM SUN
➡ 1.8 billion miles (2.9 billion km)

LENGTH OF YEAR
➡ 84.07 Earth years

LENGTH OF DAY
➡ 17 Earth hours, 14 minutes

AVERAGE TEMPERATURE
➡ -371°F (-224°C)

SURFACE DETAILS
➡ No solid surface

NUMBER OF MOONS
➡ 27

Uranus is the coldest planet in the entire solar system. It is a bit different than the other planets: It's tipped over to the point that it is rotating on its side. This is because of Uranus's huge tilt. Earth has a tilt of about 23.5 degrees. Uranus has a tilt of 99 degrees. That's a big difference!

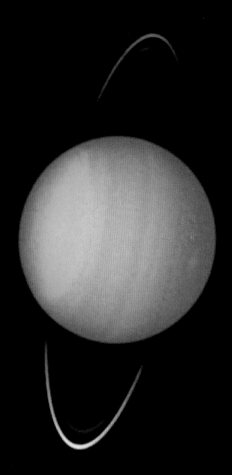

WHY IS URANUS TIPPED OVER?

Astronomers believe Uranus spins on its side for one of two reasons.

1. One theory is that billions of years ago, as the planets were forming, a large object crashed into Uranus. The crash was so powerful it knocked Uranus onto its side.

2. The other theory is that a large moon may have caused the tilt. The moon was slowly pulled away from Uranus by another large planet. The result? The gravitational pull of this moon, traveling away from Uranus, tilted the planet.

WHY IS URANUS COLDER THAN NEPTUNE?

If Neptune is farthest from the Sun, then how is Uranus colder? There are three reasons for its deep chill.

1. Uranus doesn't make its own heat. It gives off less heat than it absorbs from the Sun. The other planets in the Jovian family give off more heat than they absorb from the Sun.

2. Scientists believe when it got knocked over billions of years ago, Uranus lost a great deal of its internal heat.

3. Uranus can't hold in its heat. One year on Uranus lasts 84 Earth years, and each hemisphere spends half that time in daylight and the other in total darkness, so the Sun can only heat up one pole at a time.

13 RINGS

Astronomers discovered rings on Uranus in 1977 in phases. Through giant telescopes, astronomers initially found nine rings around the planet. Photographs sent back from the Voyager spacecraft in the 1980s showed two additional rings around the planet. Then between 2003 and 2005, the Hubble Space Telescope discovered two more rings for a total of 13 rings around Uranus.

STELLAR STATS
NEPTUNE

NAME
➡ Neptune, named for the Roman god of the sea

NICKNAME
➡ Oceanus or The Blue Planet

DIAMETER
➡ 29,297 miles (47,149 km)

MASS
➡ 17 times Earth's mass

GRAVITY COMPARED TO EARTH
➡ 1.12

NUMBER OF RINGS
➡ 6

DISTANCE FROM EARTH
➡ 2.7 billion miles (4.3 billion km)

DISTANCE FROM SUN
➡ 2.8 billion miles (4.5 billion km)

LENGTH OF YEAR
➡ 164.81 Earth years

LENGTH OF DAY
➡ 16 Earth hours, 7 minutes

AVERAGE TEMPERATURE
➡ -360°F (-218°C)

SURFACE DETAILS
➡ Probably icy with craters

NUMBER OF MOONS
➡ 13

If you were to see Neptune up close, you would find storms on the surface and freezing cold winds. Neptune is a large planet. How large? If Earth was a nickel, Neptune would be the size of a baseball. It appears blue because of its hydrogen-methane atmosphere. It also has white clouds stretched out all around it.

NEPTUNE UP CLOSE

On August 25, 1989, the Voyager 2 spacecraft flew by Neptune and delivered close-up images.

THAT'S ASTRONOMICAL!

Neptune and Uranus are the two windiest planets in the solar system. Astronomers have measured winds on Neptune moving at 1,300 miles per hour (2,100 kph) and Uranus at 580 miles per hour (930 kph).

Neptune's clouds, blown by the wind

EUREKA!

It wasn't a telescope that discovered Neptune, but mathematics. The British mathematician John Couch Adams and the French astronomer Urbain Le Verrier used math to predict the location of planet Neptune. Each observed that Uranus was speeding up and slowing down, and realized that this could be due to the pull of another planet. They came to this realization independently. They calculated where Neptune was located. However, it wasn't until astronomer Johann Galle decided to test this theory and he observed Neptune in 1846 that it was formally discovered.

ASK HAKEEM...

WHY ARE THE FARTHEST PLANETS THE WINDIEST?

Terrestrial planets do have winds. But the far-out Jovian planets have intense internal heat. This causes the outer planets to emit more energy than they receive from the Sun and creates greater winds. The outer planets also have atmospheres that act more like liquids, so there is no surface "roughness" to slow down the wind.

Planetary exploration missions are some of the most exciting things in the news today. Every single day astronomers, astronauts, and scientists are learning more and more about deep space! Some missions only last a year or two, but others like Voyager have gone on for decades.

WORD

Interstellar space means the space between the stars. Sometimes interstellar space is called deep space or outer space.

THE VOYAGER MISSIONS

VOYAGER 1

LAUNCHED
September 5, 1977

STATUS
Ongoing

VOYAGER 2

LAUNCHED
August 20, 1977

STATUS
Ongoing

GOAL
Voyager 1 and Voyager 2 are twin-spacecraft launched in 1977 to do the same job—investigate the Jovian planets.

V1 and V2 have visited Jupiter, Saturn, Uranus and Neptune. The Voyager Missions have now become the Voyager Interstellar Missions, with both spacecraft headed toward the boundaries of the solar system.

Voyager launch

An image of the moon Io captured by Voyager

*First image transmitted
by New Horizons*

NEW HORIZONS MISSION

LAUNCHED
January 19, 2006

STATUS
Ongoing

On July 14, 2015, New Horizons spacecraft made a flyby of Pluto. Traveling at 31,000 miles per hour (49,900 kph), it took more than nine years for New Horizons to cover 3 billion miles (4.8 billion km) to get there. It was within 7,800 miles (12,550 km) of Pluto when it photographed this planet first discovered in 1930 and previously seen as only a dot in space. No one could predict if New Horizons would survive its flyby, but it did! Here are some images it transmitted.

*July 13, 2015:
the day before the flyby*

*July 14, 2015: flyby
reveals ice mountains*

International Space Station

The International Space Station (ISS) is a human-made satellite. It's a laboratory in orbit around Earth. Sixteen countries have worked together to create this amazing experimental facility. Up to seven astronauts can work and live safely together in the space station and conduct experiments.

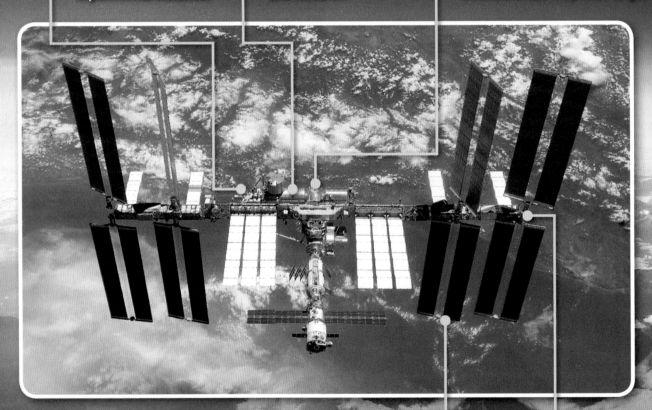

REMOTE MANIPULATOR SYSTEM
This is a robotic arm. This helps the astronauts to attach larger parts, such as the experimental modules.

EXPERIMENTAL QUARTERS
The atmosphere inside this area is just like Earth. This is where astronauts can safely conduct experiments and research.

NODES
A node is like a tunnel with air. It connects the modules with the living areas and the experimental modules. These nodes are filled with air so the astronauts can walk to and from the areas they need to go.

SOLAR ARRAYS
These panels harness sunlight to produce electricity.

TRUSS
Solar arrays can be attached to trusses. Trusses are like pillars that help hold the station together.

DELIVERING SUPPLIES

Automated cargo spacecraft are designed to bring supplies such as food and fuel to the ISS every couple of months. They don't have any crew members on board.

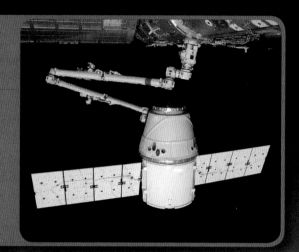

HOW LONG DO ASTRONAUTS STAY AT THE ISS?

ISS missions usually last about six months. Astronauts call their missions expeditions. Each expedition includes three to six astronauts. The astronauts come from different places, including Canada, the United States, Russia, Brazil, Japan and Europe. The longest space station expedition lasted 215 days. This record is held by American astronaut Michael Lopez-Alegria.

Michael Lopez-Alegria

HOW DO PEOPLE GET TO AND FROM THE ISS?

People usually get to the ISS in a Soyuz TMA, a fast Russian-designed spacecrafts, and it takes about a day to get there. Getting back is a much bumpier ride; the craft descends to Earth in about three hours and lands using a parachute.

BY THE NUMBERS
THE ISS

925,000
POUNDS
(420,000 kg)
Weight

357
FEET (109 km)
Length

5
MILES PER SECOND
(8 kps)
Speed it travels

90
MINUTES
Time it takes
to orbit Earth

16
TIMES IT ORBITS
Earth in a single day

In order to be an astronaut, you need a sense of adventure. Even seemingly simple things can be more difficult to do in space. Here's a look at how astronauts perform their daily tasks.

WORKING

Imagine trying to work while you're floating midair! Astronauts have to work very slowly. If they move too quickly, they can lose balance and start spinning. Space instruments and tools are tied to the astronaut as they use them so they don't float away. The instruments are designed to be bigger so the astronauts can grab them with large gloves on.

KEEPING IN SHAPE

On board the ISS, astronauts wear what they would wear on Earth, but they also have to pack workout clothes. With zero gravity in space, astronauts' muscles would weaken if they didn't exercise. So to keep their muscle mass they need to work out at least two hours per day.

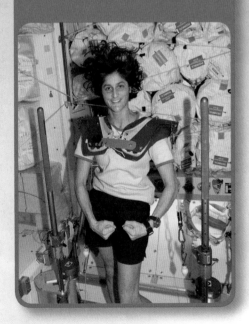

EATING

When it's time to eat, astronauts have food that is in sealed packets. Meat is irradiated prior to the missions in order to make it last longer in space. Much of the food is freeze-dried, so astronauts need to add water and heat their food in a convection oven before eating it. They attach their food containers to trays and attach the trays to their laps. Then they can eat without their dinner floating everywhere.

SLEEPING

If astronauts are floating inside the spacecraft, how do they sleep? Astronauts strap sleeping bags to the walls. They sleep vertically and secure their arms and legs to their sleeping bags.

DID YOU KNOW?

Astronauts had it tough back in the days of the Apollo missions. Before the invention of zero-gravity toilets, astronauts used suction tubes to deal with liquid waste and specialized plastic bags to deal with solid waste. This method was both uncomfortable and messy, and it led to a serious stink. Modern space facilities have air filtration systems to keep things smelling sweet.

WHAT'S THE SCOOP ON SPACE POOP?

There are special toilets and vacuums created to make waste elimination more manageable in space. Zero-gravity toilets use air pumps and fans to direct waste into storage containers. Astronauts go through practice before each mission.

WHAT IF AN ASTRONAUT GETS SICK?

Each astronaut has a special job, for medical emergencies, the crew medical officer is in charge. This astronaut not only knows first aid, but also is trained in giving injections and helping with more serious emergencies.

Spacewalking

Any time an astronaut leaves his spacecraft, it is called a space walk. Astronauts call it an EVA—an extravehicular activity. The first person to go on a space walk was Soviet cosmonaut Alexei Leonov, on March 18, 1965. His walk was ten minutes long. The longest EVA so far was 8 hours and 56 minutes, achieved by American astronauts Susan Helms and Jim Voss in 2001.

PARTS OF A SPACE SUIT

Astronauts need to dress for the elements before EVAs. They have space suits with functions designed to protect them from the dangers of space, such as radiation and space dust. The suits are equipped with oxygen so the astronauts can breathe. The temperature inside the suit is regulated so it doesn't get too hot or cold. The suit also has enough water for the astronauts to stay hydrated.

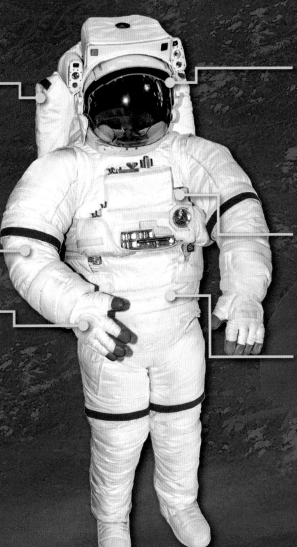

PRIMARY LIFE SUPPORT SUBSYSTEM
Worn like a backpack, this holds things needed during an EVA. It supplies oxygen and removes exhaled carbon dioxide. It also has water-cooling equipment, a fan, and a two-way radio so the astronaut can communicate.

UPPER TORSO
The top of the spacesuit that includes the hard upper torso and arm assembly.

EVA GLOVES
An astronaut must wear these in order to work. They are made so that a spacewalker can move their fingers easily. They also have heated fingertips so their hands don't freeze.

HELMET
The helmet directs and maintains oxygen needed by the astronaut. The bubble part of the helmet is covered by a visor called the extravehicular visor assembly. The visor is coated with a thick layer of gold that keeps out harmful rays from the Sun.

DISPLAYS AND CONTROL MODULE
This is the control for the life saving suits. This is there so the astronaut can operate the Primary Support Subsystem.

LOWER TORSO ASSEMBLY
This includes the pants, boots, and lower half of the waist. It comes with a movable middle, the waist bearing, which helps the astronaut turn. There are rings called D rings that attach to tethers so that a spacewalker can't float away!

MEET AN ASTRONAUT:
COLONEL CHRIS AUSTIN HADFIELD

Astronaut, engineer, and fighter pilot Chris Hadfield is a former commander of the International Space Station. In 1995, he became the only Canadian ever to board the Russian space station Mir, just three years after joining the astronaut corps. During a 2001 flight, Chris performed space walks on which he was able to leave the spacecraft and float in space freely. On his first space walk, Chris was temporarily blinded when his space suit's anti-fog solution got into his eyes. After 30 minutes, he recovered and was able to complete his mission. It was during this first space walk that he says he was able to see the world as a system. He could see the oceans on Earth; he saw Earth's magnetic field and the sunlight hitting it. He was actually walking through the aurora lights. This was a life-changing experience for Chris. As if being an astronaut wasn't cool enough, on May 12, 2013, after leaving his post as commander of the ISS, but before landing back on Earth, Chris filmed the first music video ever made in space: his version of David Bowie's song "Space Oddity." You can find this video on YouTube! In addition to all of his academic and professional accomplishments, Chris took to Twitter to share his day-to-day activities as an astronaut in space. He now has more than 1 million followers.

Microgravity

Living in space has a dramatic effect on the human body. Remember, the farther you go into space, the less gravity there is. Under the condition at microgravity (a small amount of gravity) or zero gravity, people and objects appear to be weightless. When astronauts go into space, they no longer experience the gravity we have on Earth. They can't walk or run. They only float. What else happens?

DID YOU KNOW?

You can't burp in space. Low or no gravity means no buoyancy, so there's nothing pushing gas bubbles up and out. This is why astronauts don't drink carbonated drinks on their trips to space.

WORD

Buoyancy is the ability to float in water or other fluid.

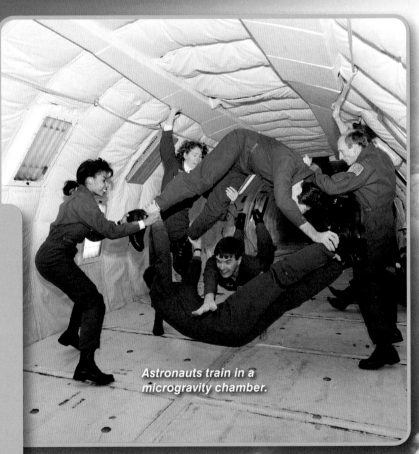

Astronauts train in a microgravity chamber.

YOUR BODY AND MICROGRAVITY

Gravity helps bones and muscles stay strong. In space, an astronaut's leg bones, hips, and spine lose their strength and ability to work properly. Calcium is released from the bones, which can cause bones to become fragile as well as cause kidney stones. Muscles can also suffer during extended space flights. Astronauts work out at least twice a day to keep their bodies healthy.

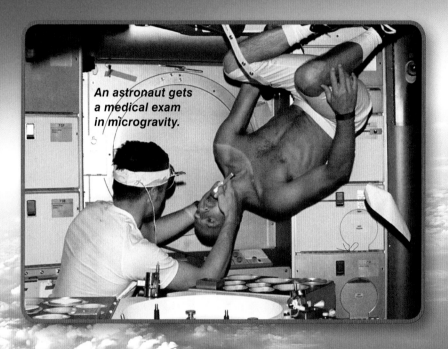

An astronaut gets a medical exam in microgravity.

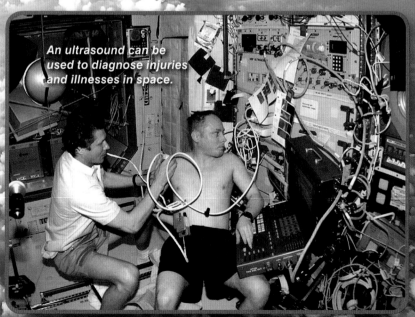

An ultrasound can be used to diagnose injuries and illnesses in space.

MICROGRAVITY FACTS

BLOOD
Without the downward pull of gravity to the lower part of the body, more blood moves to the brain and away from extremities such as hands and feet. This means astronauts often get puffy faces and feel congested.

HEART
Your heart is a muscle. It doesn't have to work as hard in space, but that is not a good thing. The heart has to be exercised, just like any other muscle.

SLEEP
In space, astronauts lose sleep. Our bodies and brains are used to a 24-hour cycle of waking and sleeping. Living on the fast-moving ISS, where the Sun rises and sets every 90 minutes, disturbs this cycle and can cause great fatigue.

HEIGHT
People are taller in space! The disks between the vertebrae of the spinal column are pushed together when you are on Earth. In space, things don't press together.

Space Experiments

Experiments help us make discoveries, test theories, and demonstrate what we already know. There are always many experiments under way on the International Space Station; here are a few interesting ones that are helping us learn more about differences--and similarities--between how things work on Earth and how they work in space.

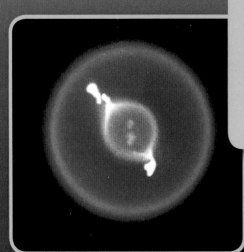

FLAME EXTINGUISHMENT EXPERIMENT (FLEX)

Fire behaves much differently in space than it does on Earth. Without gravity, hot air expands but doesn't move upward and flames are dome-shaped. FLEX helped scientists discover that flames in space burn at a lower temperature, at a slower rate, and with less oxygen than on Earth.

ROBONAUT

A dexterous humanoid-type robot—one that can do the kinds of things people do with their hands—could take over repetitive or dangerous tasks inside and outside the space station. R2, the latest version of Robonaut, has long legs that were built on Earth and attached to the robot on the ISS.

3-D PRINTING

With the help of 3-D printing technology, astronauts could have a working machine shop in space. This means they could make parts when they needed them, rather than waiting for a delivery from Earth. A 3-D printer has already been operated successfully on the space station, and more experiments are under way.

ASTRO-SPIDERS

NASA sent two golden orb spiders—Gladys and Esmeralda—into space to see how they would behave in microgravity. Scientists observed that the spiders behaved just as naturally in space as on Earth. However, on Earth these spiders spin three-dimensional asymmetric webs, but in space their webs were more circular. Unfortunately, Esmeralda didn't survive the trip back to Earth, but Gladys did—or rather, Gladstone. Upon the return, scientists discovered she was a he.

AT A GLANCE

ASTEROIDS
➡ Millions of icy rocks in the Asteroid Belt
➡ Left over from 4.6 billion years ago

SPACE JUNK
➡ Litter, including debris from missions and defunct satellites, orbits Earth

METEOROIDS AND METEORS
➡ Space rocks in motion, often formed from comet tails
➡ Meteor showers are burning meteors we call shooting stars

THE KUIPER BELT
➡ Home to dwarf planets including Pluto

THE OORT CLOUD
➡ Located at the far reaches of our Solar System
➡ Vast cloud where most comets orginate

ROSETTA MISSION
➡ A successful mission to land on a comet

A meteor falling over ALMA Observatory

Asteroids, Meteors, Comets and More

Asteroids, meteors, and comets are flying objects made of ice and rock. They orbit the Sun and sometimes get close enough to Earth for us to see. They are often grouped together, are irregularly shaped and not big enough to be planets, and some have even crashed into Earth. Continue farther into space and we find the distant Kuiper Belt—home to Pluto and other dwarf planets—and the Oort Cloud, active places that can tell scientists what the early solar system was like.

The Asteroid Belt

NICKNAME
➡ The Main Belt

DISCOVERED
➡ The first discovery in the Asteroid Belt was Ceres, in 1801

MASS
➡ 4% of the mass of the Moon

AVERAGE DISTANCE BETWEEN BELT OBJECTS
➡ 600,000 miles (967,000 km)

DISTANCE FROM SUN
➡ 3.2 Astronomical Units

LARGEST KNOWN OBJECT
➡ Dwarf planet Ceres

Asteroids are space objects that orbit the Sun. They are made of rocks and metals. Asteroids are left over from 4.6 billion years ago when the solar system was formed. In fact, some scientists believe that the asteroids that hit Earth delivered the minerals needed to sustain life on our planet.

Most asteroids are in the vast area between the orbits of Mars and Jupiter. They orbit the Sun in a doughnut-shaped region called the Asteroid Belt. It holds more than 200 asteroids larger than 60 miles in diameter, including dwarf planet Ceres, and millions of smaller ones. Comets have also been discovered in the Asteroid Belt.

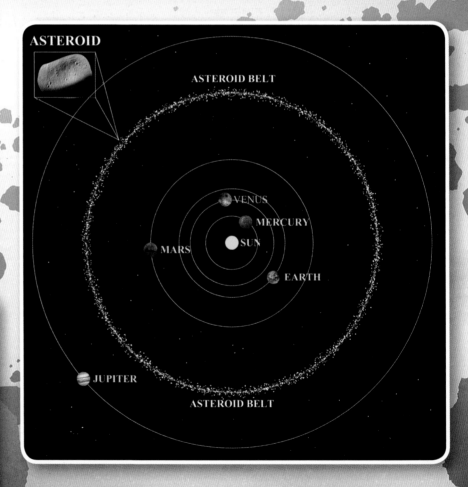

ASTEROID

ASTEROID BELT

VENUS

MERCURY

SUN

MARS

EARTH

JUPITER

ASTEROID BELT

Ceres is 598 miles (962 km) in diameter. Photographed by NASA's Dawn spacecraft in May 2015.

THAT'S ASTRONOMICAL!

Asteroids are rich in valuable minerals. It is estimated that the entire Asteroid Belt would be worth $100 billion for each person on Earth.

WORD

One **Astronomical Unit** (AU) equals the distance of the Sun from Earth. When astronomers talk about deep space, like the Kuiper Belt or the Oort Cloud, they use AUs to discuss distance.

NEAR EARTH ASTEROID RENDEZVOUS (NEAR)

LAUNCHED
February 17, 1996

STATUS
Last transmission to Earth: February 28, 2001

NEAR's goal was to find out more about how asteroids originated and what clues they hold about the evolution of the solar system. The NEAR Shoemaker was the first space probe to orbit and perform an in-depth look at an asteroid. Although the orbiter wasn't designed to do so, it landed safely on the asteroid Eros. It continued to transmit data for two weeks after landing.

UNEXPECTED DISCOVERY

Ida is an oddly shaped asteroid with many craters. In 1993, the Galileo spacecraft came within 1,500 miles (2,414 km) of Ida and found it had a moon. They named it Dactyl. Dactyl is the first natural satellite of an asteroid ever discovered.

Strange Debris

Traveling in orbit are about 50,000 pieces of debris. Some of it is very large, such as burnt-out rockets and satellites, some is materials intentionally discarded by spacecraft missions, and other pieces are things lost during spacewalks. Space debris travels very fast—at 18,000 miles per hour (29,000 kph), and collisions with this fast-moving debris could harm or even destroy a spacecraft.

WHAT'S THE SOLUTION TO SPACE POLLUTION?

Low-orbiting space junk may fall to Earth, usually disintegrating when entering the Earth's atmosphere. Higher-flying debris may take decades to disintegrate. Space agencies such as NASA are working to control orbital debris on current and future missions. NASA's Orbital Debris Program Office looks for ways to reduce orbital debris and get rid of debris already in space.

HOW MUCH SPACE JUNK IS THERE?

The United States Space Surveillance Network tracks thousands of man-made objects, including active and inactive satellites and debris the size of a baseball and larger. But that's just a fraction of the amount of junk orbiting Earth.

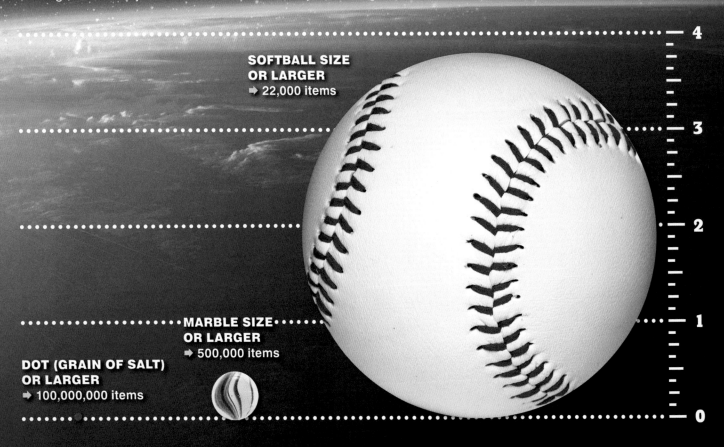

SOFTBALL SIZE OR LARGER
➡ 22,000 items

MARBLE SIZE OR LARGER
➡ 500,000 items

DOT (GRAIN OF SALT) OR LARGER
➡ 100,000,000 items

4

3

2

1

0

HOW DO ASTRONAUTS STAY SAFE FROM ORBITAL DEBRIS?

➡ NASA keeps track of the larger debris so spacecraft crews are aware of their location. This helps astronauts dodge the larger pieces.

➡ When astronauts are working on the ISS, they are protected by the heavy shield around the ISS and can survive bumps with pieces of debris.

➡ Multiple layers inside their spacesuits help astronauts withstand any run-ins with small space debris.

THE STRANGEST DEBRIS IN SPACE

SPATULA
In 2006, during Discovery's flight to the ISS, astronaut Piers Sellers lost his spatula while making repairs to a heat-shield.

TOOL BAG
Astronaut Heidemarie Stefanyshyn-Piper lost her tool bag while on a spacewalk in November 2008. It was a 30-pound bag packed with tools estimated at a value of $100,000.

GLOVE
The very first American spacewalker, Edward White, let go of a glove during the 1965 Gemini 4 flight. The glove stayed in orbit for about a month before it burned upon entering Earth's atmosphere.

TANK OF AMMONIA
This was an intentional discard. In July 2007, NASA wanted to lighten a spacecraft's load on the way back to Earth and told the astronauts to throw out an unneeded 1,400-pound (635kg) tank of ammonia. It took more than a year for it to hit Earth's atmosphere and burn up.

URINE
The urine produced by astronauts has been dumped overboard. Once the urine meets the cold vacuum of space, it freezes into tiny crystals and floats around as debris. The ISS has a Water Recovery System that recycles everything from water used for bathing to urine and sweat.

CAMERA
In June 2007, astronaut Suni Williams's camera came untethered and floated away during an EVA.

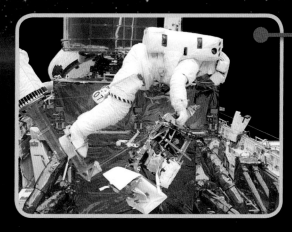

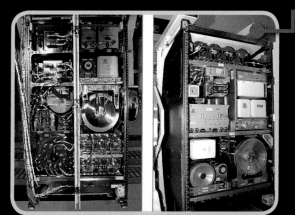

Meteoroids travel around the Sun in different orbits and at varying speeds. When they enter Earth's atmosphere, they become meteors; their speed heats the gases in the atmosphere, creating bright streaks in the sky. We often call these streaks of light shooting stars, but they aren't stars at all.

METEOR SHOWERS: FIREWORKS IN THE NIGHT SKY!

Meteor showers occur when a comet traveling close to the Sun sheds debris. The debris—meteoroids, most of which are smaller than a grain of sand—are left in the path the comet was traveling. When Earth passes through the comet's orbit, meteoroids enter Earth's atmosphere and burn up, creating meteor showers.

Some meteor showers happen at the same time each year, and on a clear night you can see hundreds of shooting stars in the sky.

➜ The Quadrantids occur from the end of December to mid-January, and peak night viewing is January 3–4

➜ The Lyrids occur in late April, and peak night viewing is April 22–23

➜ The Perseids occur in mid-August, and peak night viewing is August 11–13

➜ The Geminids occur in early December, and peak night viewing is December 13–14

GALACTIC FACT

The fastest meteoroids travel through space at 26 miles per second (42 kps).

Geminid meteors streak across the sky in Iowa

107

WHICH IS IT?

ASTEROID
Chunk of rock that comes from the Asteroid Belt and orbits the Sun.

METEOROID
Small piece of debris from an asteroid or comet orbiting the Sun.

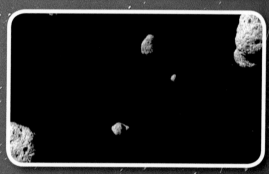

SHOOTING STAR
Streak of light that occurs when a meteor burns up.

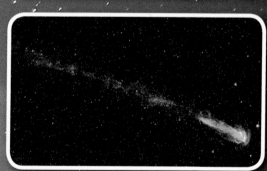

METEORITE
A rock that falls from space and lands on Earth.

Meteorite Crashes

Meteorite impacts are one of the most destructive forces in space. They have left ancient scars on Earth and may have even caused mass extinction. But they may also have delivered chemicals to the planet in its early years, seeds that allowed Earth to grow.

BARRINGER METEORITE CRATER

This tremendous impact crater in Arizona was created more than 50,000 years ago. It's almost a mile across and 570 feet (170 m). Scientists believe it was created by a meteorite at least 160 feet (49 m) deep. The impact of the meteorite was 150 times the force of an atomic bomb. Apollo astronauts trained here in the 1960s, to prepare for their moon landing.

VREDEFORT DOME

The biggest impact crater on Earth is located in Vredefort, South Africa. It is 186 miles (299 km) wide and is estimated to be 2 billion years old. The crater was caused by a meteorite that measured about six miles (9.6 km) wide. The crater is mostly eroded away but a bit of the dome is left.

WHY AREN'T THERE MORE CRATERS?

There are only about 120 meteorite craters on Earth, but scientists believe there have been more crashes. They think that earthquakes and erupting volcanoes, which cause Earth to "heal," have erased the craters.

The Ouarkziz Impact Crater in Algeria was formed less than 70 million years ago.

ASK HAKEEM...

COULD EARTH BE WIPED OUT BY A METEOR, ASTEROID, OR COMET?

In tens of millions of years, yes, there's a chance that this could happen. As for what object it could be, there are far more comets than asteroids or meteors, but comets must travel from the outer reaches of the solar system. Near-Earth Asteroids are closer, but there are fewer of them. So, scientists don't know exactly which one of these objects could land on Earth, but it won't be anytime soon.

CHICXULUB CRATER

Dinosaurs died off 66 million years ago, and no one knows exactly why this occurred. One theory is that a comet, asteroid, or meteorite impact caused the end of the dinosaurs. Such a destructive crash would have caused a huge crater. In 1990, scientists found the Chicxulub Crater on the edge of the Yucatán Peninsula, which was dated to that exact prehistoric time period. Scientists are planning to drill deep into the crater to look for ancient evidence from the time of the mass extinction.

Chicxulub impact crater, which is at the bottom of the Gulf of Mexico (artist's rendering)

The Kuiper Belt

The Kuiper Belt is a vast, cold and distant area of the outer solar system, loaded with over 70,000—and possibly as many as a million—rocky, icy, and shiny objects. Dwarf planets like Pluto call the Kuiper Belt home. Objects in the Kuiper Belt are like fossils that geologists find on Earth in that they tell a story about how the area evolved.

DWARF PLANETS

There are four known dwarf planets in the Kuiper Belt: Pluto, Eris, Makemake, and Haumea. Scientists believe there may be as many as one hundred dwarf planets in space, but there are only five officially recognized dwarf planets in our solar system (including Ceres in the Asteroid Belt). These dwarf planets have several things in common:

➡ Orbit the Sun

➡ Are smaller than planets

➡ Are round

➡ There are no known rings around dwarf planets

➡ Many, but not all, dwarf planets have moons

➡ Are not moons of other planets

➡ Have orbits that may intersect with others'

STELLAR STATS
THE EDGEWORTH-KUIPER BELT

NICKNAME
➡ The Kuiper Belt

DISCOVERED
➡ August 30, 1992

MASS
➡ One tenth of Earth's mass

NUMBER OF OBJECTS
➡ 70,000 and counting

DISTANCE FROM SUN
➡ 30–50 Astronomical Units

LARGEST OBJECT
➡ Pluto

ORIGINS OF THE KUIPER BELT

Astronomers believe that the objects found here are icy bits left over from explosions during the formation of the early Solar System, and that they were pushed out to the edge of the solar system by the gravity of the gas giants, Jupiter and Saturn. Here are some of the largest Kuiper Belt Objects (KBOs), which includes dwarf planets Pluto, Eris, Makemake, and Haumea. Distant KBOs Sedna and Quaoar were both discovered in the early 2000s and may one day be determined to be dwarf planets, as well. (The small objects shown are moons.)

Weywot

QUAOAR

SEDNA

Hi'iaka, Namaka

HAUMEA

MAKEMAKE

Dysnomia

ERIS

Charon, Hydra, Nix

PLUTO

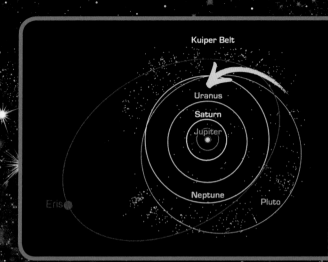

WHAT HAPPENED TO PLUTO?

Pluto is one-fifth the size of Earth and 2.8 billion miles (4.5 billion km) from the Sun. It has five moons, and from its discovery in 1930 until 2006 it was considered a planet. It lost its place as the tiniest planet in our solar system when scientists determined it didn't meet the new criteria to be called a planet.

In order to make the grade and become an official planet, a celestial body must:

1. Orbit the Sun

2. Be round in shape

3. Clear the orbit of another planet

Pluto meets the criteria for the first two, but not the third. Pluto's orbit overlaps with the path of Neptune. This makes Pluto a dwarf planet.

Pluto appears as a bright spot in this photo from March 1930, a month after it was discovered by astronomer Clyde W. Tombaugh.

NEW HORIZONS
PLUTO-KUIPER BELT MISSION

LAUNCHED
January 2006

STATUS
Ongoing

NASA launched New Horizons in January 2006 to understand the icy worlds of Pluto and the Kuiper Belt. The first images of Pluto from the New Horizons mission were released in July 2015. NASA's New Horizons team will map this distant world and its moons for the first time.

New Horizons photos from July 2015 have revealed the dwarf planet in far greater detail.

The Oort Cloud

Keep going . . . keep going . . . until you reach the Oort Cloud. This is a theoretical place we can't yet observe at the outer reaches of our solar system. Scientists believe this is where most comets come from. Objects inside the cloud are mostly made of water ice, ammonia, and methane. There are an estimated 2 trillion icy objects inside this chilly cloud.

STELLAR STATS

THE ÖPIK-OORT CLOUD

NICKNAME
➡ The Oort Cloud

DISCOVERED
➡ In 1943, astronomer Kenneth Edgeworth thought there was a supply or reservoir of comets beyond the planets. In 1950, Jan Oort suggested there is a large cloud of comets at the edge of the solar system.

DISTANCE FROM SUN
➡ 1,000–100,000 Astronomical Units

ESTIMATED NUMBER OF OBJECTS
➡ 2 trillion

WHAT—AND WHERE—IS IT?

Astronomers think that the particles in the Oort Cloud were scattered into space by the powerful gravity of the Jovian planets. They think the Oort Cloud has two areas: the spherical outer Oort cloud and a disc-shaped inner cloud called the Hills Cloud. No spacecraft has seen the Oort cloud and there are no current plans to venture that far into space, but one day we may be able to see and learn more.

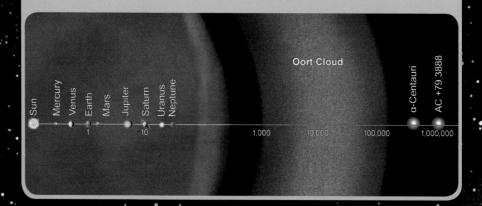

WHAT IS A COMET?

Scientists think comets are relics from the origins of the solar system. There is evidence that comets played an important role in the development of the planets. For instance, scientists believe that comets brought much of the water to today's oceans. Comets could have provided chemicals for the soil to produce plant life on Earth.

A comet has several parts. The central part of a comet—often described as being like a dirty snowball—is the nucleus. It's made of rock, ice, gas, and dust. As the comet moves closer to the Sun, the nucleus begins to melt and a cloud of water vapor surrounds the comet. The cloud is called a coma and it can actually grow to be 50,000 miles (80,500 km) wide. After the coma is formed, the comet grows a tail, which can stretch out to 600,000 miles (967,000 km).

FAMOUS COMETS

HALLEY'S COMET

is named after English astronomer Edmond Halley, who figured out the comet had a repeating path. Records of scientists observing Halley's Comet go back thousands of years. It can be seen with the naked eye from Earth every 75 years or so. It was last seen in 1986 and will return around 2061.

SHOEMAKER-LEVY 9

was a comet that crashed into Jupiter in 1994. That crash had the force of 6,000 gigatons (6 quintillion kg) of TNT. A fireball rose 1,800 miles (2,897 km) above the Jovian clouds. The comet had more than 20 impacts, and the collisions were visible through the Hubble and other telescopes on Earth and the Galileo spacecarft.

HALE-BOPP

was one of the most viewed comets in history. In the 1990s, the comet was close to Earth and could be seen in the northern sky for more than 18 months. It was 1,000 times brighter than Halley's Comet and had twin blue and white tails that were easily seen.

Gas ion tail

Dust tail

Nucleus

Landing on a Comet

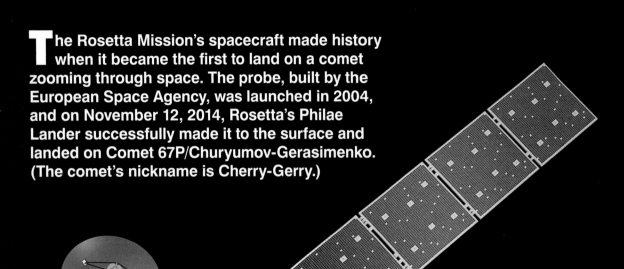

The Rosetta Mission's spacecraft made history when it became the first to land on a comet zooming through space. The probe, built by the European Space Agency, was launched in 2004, and on November 12, 2014, Rosetta's Philae Lander successfully made it to the surface and landed on Comet 67P/Churyumov-Gerasimenko. (The comet's nickname is Cherry-Gerry.)

HOW DID IT LAND?

Rosetta had to make three flybys of Earth, and one of Mars, just to work up enough speed to whiz by Jupiter to meet the comet. Jupiter is huge and has a large gravitational pull, so Rosetta needed enough momentum so that it wouldn't get sucked into Jupiter's orbit.

A comet nucleus has very low gravity, so the lander was outfitted with harpoons. The landing was softer than expected, and the harpoons didn't deploy. The lander had ice screws built into its feet to attach itself to the comet's surface.

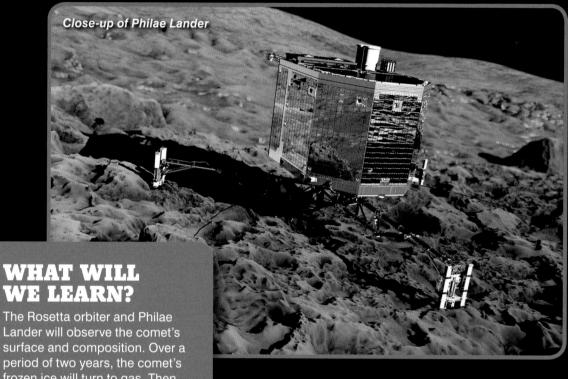

Close-up of Philae Lander

WHAT WILL WE LEARN?

The Rosetta orbiter and Philae Lander will observe the comet's surface and composition. Over a period of two years, the comet's frozen ice will turn to gas. Then scientists will see for the first time a close-up view of the change that takes place as the ice in space is warmed by the Sun.

Relying on solar panels to power the lander, it was dormant for several months when it didn't have enough sunlight. It began transmitting again in June 2015.

Close-up of Comet 67P/Churyumov-Gerasimenko

AT A GLANCE

LIFE CYCLE

➡ How a star is born, ages, and dies depends on its mass.

➡ The less mass a star has, the longer its life. The smallest stars can last for more than a trillion years.

FORMING STARS

➡ All stars start out as nebulas, graduate to protostars, and become main sequence stars.

MATURE STARS

➡ Stars lose more and more mass as they age.

➡ Main sequence stars grow to be giant stars.

DYING STARS

➡ A low mass star becomes a planetary nebula and white dwarf.

➡ The most massive stars explode at the end of their lives.

THE ELECTROMAGNETIC SPECTRUM

➡ Energy exists in space as well as on Earth.

➡ Energy travels in short and long waves.

➡ Some energy is visible, and some is invisible.

Super Stars

Stars may seem like tiny diamonds glittering in the sky. But in fact, stars are huge, bright balls of hot plasma. They only look small because they are so far away.

Nobody knows exactly how many stars are in the universe, but astronomers estimate between 200 and 400 billion just in our galaxy, the Milky Way. And there are hundreds of billions of other galaxies in the universe, which may have even more stars than we do.

Star Qualities

There are many different kinds of stars. They vary in size, temperature, color, and brightness. The closer a star is to Earth, the larger it is, or the hotter it is, the brighter it appears in our sky. Some are smaller than Earth, and others are gigantic—hundreds of times larger than our Sun. Astronomers carefully study each kind of star and group them based on their similarities.

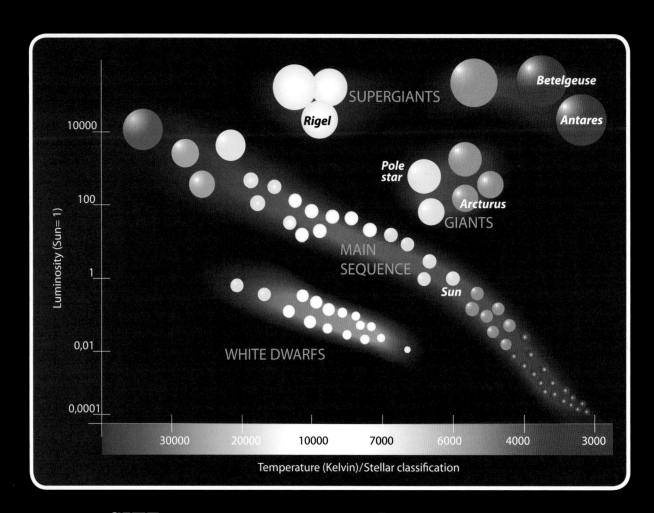

SIZE

Compared to our Sun, which is an average-sized star, diameters of stars can be 450 times smaller to over 1,000 times larger.

TEMPERATURE

Stars are superhot! Surface temperatures can range from 5,430°F (3,000°C) to over 90,000°F (50,000°C). The temperature of a star depends on its mass and age. High mass stars burn faster and hotter than low mass stars.

COLOR

Stars are different colors depending on their temperature. From lowest to highest temperature, stars can be brown, red, orange, yellow, white, or blue.

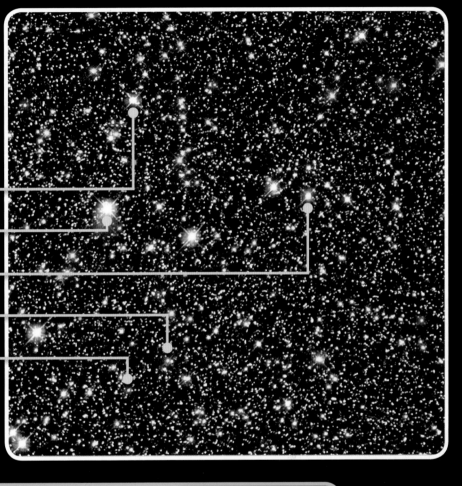

BLUE

WHITE

YELLOW

ORANGE

RED

THE 10 BRIGHTEST STARS IN EARTH'S SKY

	Star Name	Constellation	Light-Years Away
10.	Betelgeuse	Orion	640
9.	Procyon	Canis Minor	11.4
8.	Rigel	Orion	0.12
7.	Capella	Auriga	41
6.	Vega	Lyra	25
5.	Arcturus	Boötes	34
4.	Alpha Centauri	Centaurus	4.3
3.	Canopus	Carina	74
2.	Sirius	Canis Major	8.6
1.	The Sun	Zodiac	.000016

BETELGEUSE

WORD

Kelvin is a scale that astronomers often use to measure temperatures in space. Fahrenheit and Celsius are other scales that measure temperature. 1,000 kelvins equals 1,340°F (727°C).

Life Cycle of a Star

Stars may appear to be permanent objects in the night sky. But stars have a life cycle: they are born, grow larger as they burn their fuel, and die. Stars are born in huge molecular clouds of gas and dust called nebulas. How long a star shines depends on its size—the less mass it has, the longer its life. Low-mass stars burn fuel more slowly and may last billions or trillions of years. High-mass stars use up their fuel more quickly and may live only a few million years. The diagram shows how stars live and die.

A STAR IS BORN

NEBULA
New stars form in giant molecular clouds of gas and dust than spin, creating a cocoon.

PATH #1:

PROTOSTAR
As the dust and gas spin, the cocoon shrinks and a protostar forms.

Billions of Years

A STAR GETS OLDER

MAIN SEQUENCE STAR
A core is formed and energy comes out of the star as heat and light.

GIANT STAR
Hydrogen fuel that powers the star begins to burn out, the star expands, cools, and changes color.

A STAR DIES
IT EXPANDS AND FADES AWAY

PLANETARY NEBULA
These are created when a dying star releases gas and dust.

WHITE DWARF
The star core left behind becomes a white dwarf.

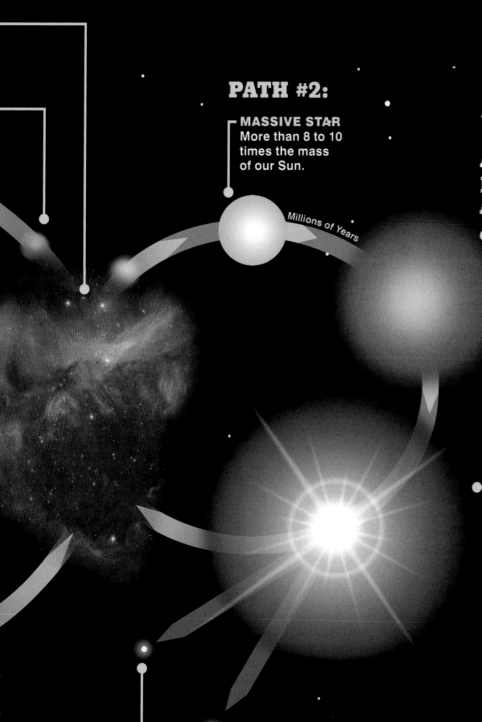

PATH #2:

MASSIVE STAR
More than 8 to 10 times the mass of our Sun.

Millions of Years

A STAR DIES
IT EXPANDS
AND EXPLODES!

SUPERGIANT
Similar to a giant star, only bigger. They are so large because they stretch out as they burn helium.

SUPERNOVA
A massive star has a violent end. Its remains scatter around space in a huge explosion.

BLACK HOLE
Has such strong gravity that anything crossing its event horizon—including light—cannot escape.

NEUTRON STAR
May be left after a massive star explodes. Neutron stars are small and compact, but very heavy.

When a star dies, it may leave behind a nebula. *Nebula* is the Latin word for "cloud," and a nebula is a cloud made from space dust and gas. The unique thing about a nebula is that it can be both a birthplace of new stars and the remains of old ones.

DIFFERENT TYPES OF NEBULAS

Nebulas are enormous—they can be hundreds of light-years across. They come in various shapes and sizes. Some release light, some reflect light, and some block light. Here are four categories.

EMISSION NEBULA

Releases gases with high radiation, similar to neon light, causing the nebula to glow. Emission nebulas are usually fuzzy pink or red clouds.

BUBBLE NEBULA

TRIFID NEBULA

REFLECTION NEBULA

Reflects the light from a group of nearby stars. These nebulas tend to look like fuzzy blue clouds.

DARK NEBULA

Blocks the light from objects behind it. These nebulas look like dark regions of dust.

HORSEHEAD NEBULA

PLANETARY NEBULA

A shell of gas made by a star as it comes to the end of its life. (They have nothing to do with actual planets. They got the name because when one was first discovered, through a telescope it looked like a planet.)

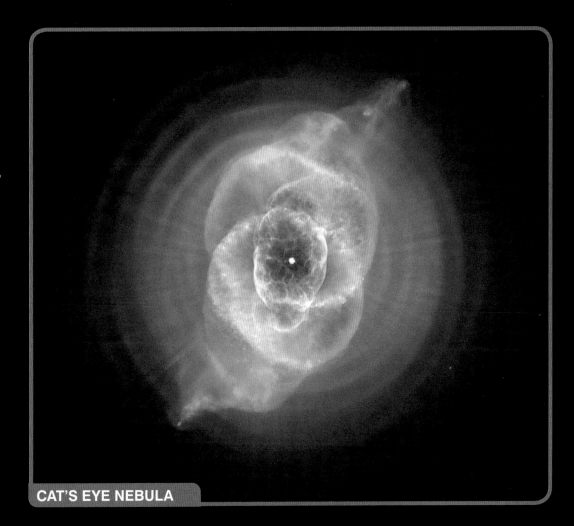

CAT'S EYE NEBULA

SPOOKY SPACE

Some nebulas have spooky names. Take a look and see if you can spot the outline of the face shape in the this image.

WITCH HEAD NEBULA

Eagle Nebula

One of the most breathtaking images ever taken by the Hubble Space Telescope is of the Eagle Nebula, also known as the cluster M16. It looks like an eagle swooping down to catch its prey.

The Eagle Nebula is a huge cloud where stars are being born. New stars have been forming in its cocoons over hundreds of millions of years.

STELLAR STATS
EAGLE NEBULA

CATEGORY
➡ Emission nebula

LOCATION
➡ Serpens constellation

AGE
➡ 5.5 million years old

DISTANCE FROM EARTH
➡ 7,000 light-years

SIZE
➡ 20 light-years across in length; the pillars are 2 to 3 light-years long

THE PILLARS OF CREATION

These stunning columns, known as the "Pillars of Creation" are located in the Eagle Nebula.

CLOSE-UP OF THE PILLARS OF CREATION

GALACTIC FACT

The hottest stars in this cluster inside the Eagle Nebula are 10,000 times brighter than the Sun.

Over time stars change. The main sequence stage in a star's development is the stage during which the star is most active—it is releasing energy. This stage lasts most of a star's life.

MAIN SEQUENCE STARS

A protostar becomes a main sequence star when its core temperature reaches 10 million Kelvins. Most of the stars in the sky, including our Sun, are main sequence stars. And most have small mass and develop into a Yellow Dwarf or Red Dwarf.

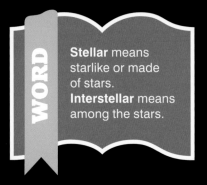

WORD

Stellar means starlike or made of stars.
Interstellar means among the stars.

STELLAR STATS
YELLOW DWARF STARS

WELL-KNOWN YELLOW DWARFS
➡ The Sun, Alpha Centauri

LIFE SPAN
➡ 10 billion years

TEMPERATURE
➡ 10,340°F (5,727°C)

MASS
➡ 1.2 times that of the Sun

COLOR
➡ White to yellow

ALPHA CENTAURI

PROXIMA CENTAURI

STELLAR STATS
RED DWARF STARS

WELL-KNOWN RED DWARFS
➡ Proxima Centauri and Barnard's Star

LIFE SPAN
➡ Up to 10 trillion years

TEMPERATURE
➡ 5,000°F (2,760°C)

MASS
➡ 0.5 times that of the Sun

COLOR
➡ Orange to red

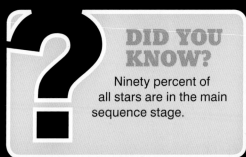

DID YOU KNOW?
Ninety percent of all stars are in the main sequence stage.

BY THE NUMBERS
NEW STARS

7

NEW STARS
are created in the Milky Way every year.

Giant stars are old, large stars. They are approaching the beginning of the end of their life cycles, and can be red or blue. How do main sequence stars become giants? As a star begins to run out of fuel, its core gets hotter and hotter. It starts to push out the layers that surround its core. The star expands, taking up much more space than when it was first born.

RED GIANTS

As a star ages, it expands—a red giant usually grows 100 times larger than it was at birth and becomes cooler over time. An example of a red giant is Aldebaran, the "eye of the bull" in the Taurus constellation.

Aldebaran

GALACTIC FACT

In several billion years, the Sun will turn into a red giant star. At that point, it will not be able to support life on Earth—but more distant parts of the Solar System could warm up.

Like many red giant stars, Aldebaran has an orange hue.

BLUE GIANTS

Blue giant stars are very hot, very massive stars. Rigel, a blue giant in the Orion constellation, is about 8 million years old. Over the next few million years, it will swell up, become a supergiant, and explode. When that happens, Rigel will be the brightest object in the night sky after the Moon.

Betelguese

Rigel

Rigel shines 40,000 times brighter than the Sun.

ASK HAKEEM...

WILL WE EVER BE ABLE TO TRAVEL TO THE STARS?

Scientists—including me!—are working on that right now. It could take more than 100 years for humans to be able to travel to the stars, but Mae Jemison, the first African-American woman to travel into space, and I are working on a project called the 100-Year Starship to enable interstellar travel.

Supergiant stars are the largest known stars in the universe. Some are almost as large as our entire solar system. When supergiants die, they don't become white dwarfs. Their mass is so great, they explode into supernovas, and their remnants eventually become neutron stars or black holes.

HOW GIANT ARE THEY?

If you put the Sun next to a supergiant, you would barely be able to see the Sun. And, these stars are so incredibly bright that if a planet were to orbit one, it would always be daytime on that planet.

STELLAR STATS
BETELGEUSE

NAME
➡ Also known as Alpha Orionis

DIAMETER
➡ 850 million miles (1.4 billion km)

MASS
➡ 20 times that of the Sun

AGE
➡ 10 million years old

DISCOVERED
➡ 1867, by Sir John Herschel

LOCATION
➡ About 640 light-years from Earth

SURFACE TEMPERATURE
➡ 5,840°F (3,227°C)

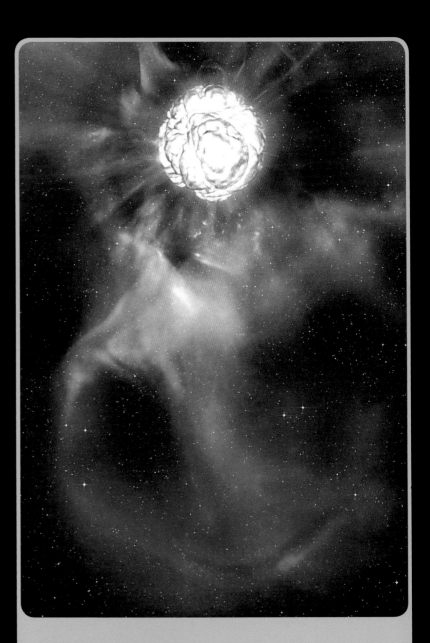

BETELGEUSE

Betelgeuse, part of the Orion constellation, is an example of a red supergiant. It is 20 times as big as the Sun and is one of the brightest stars in the night sky. You can see Betelgeuse at night throughout most of the year.

R136A1

R136A1

Of all of the massive stars, this is the one to beat—R136A1 is the most massive and most luminous star ever found. Although it was first observed in 1960, it wasn't until 2010 when the technology of the Hubble and the Very Large Telescopes (VLT) that scientists were able to truly identify this star and determine it is at least 9 million times brighter than the Sun.

STELLAR STATS
R136A1

DIAMETER
➜ 15 million miles
   (24 million km)

MASS
➜ 265 times that of the Sun

AGE
➜ 2 million years old

DISCOVERED
➜ 2010, by British astrophysicist
   Paul Crowther

LOCATION
➜ 165,000 light-years from
   Earth, Dorado Constellation

SURFACE TEMPERATURE
➜ 95,000°F (52,750°C)

STELLAR STATS
ETA CARINAE

DIAMETER
➜ 1 billion miles
   (1.6 billion km)

MASS
➜ 120 times that of the Sun

AGE
➜ 3 million years old

DISCOVERED
➜ 1677 by British astronomer
   Edmund Halley

LOCATION
➜ 8,000 light-years from
   Earth, Carina Constellation

SURFACE TEMPERATURE
➜ 72,000°F (40,000°C)

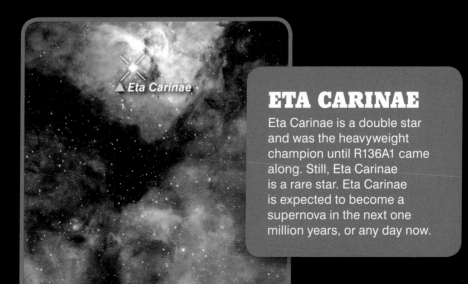

▲ Eta Carinae

ETA CARINAE

Eta Carinae is a double star and was the heavyweight champion until R136A1 came along. Still, Eta Carinae is a rare star. Eta Carinae is expected to become a supernova in the next one million years, or any day now.

What happens when low-mass stars come to the ends of their lives? When a red giant star loses its gravitational pull and its shell is ejected due to thermal pulses emanating from its core. What's left behind is a planetary nebula and a white dwarf. This will be the ultimate fate of most main sequence stars, including the Sun.

PLANETARY NEBULAS

A star sheds its outer gas shell, which becomes a nebula. Planetary nebulas are some of the most stunning objects in space. But they don't last long—they remain for only about 30,000 years. Astronomers have discovered about 2,000 planetary nebulas so far, but they believe there are at least 10,000 in our Milky Way alone.

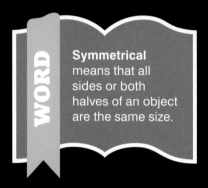

WORD

Symmetrical means that all sides or both halves of an object are the same size.

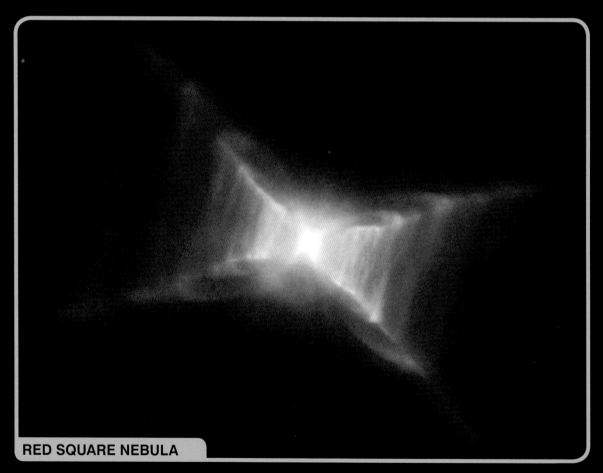

RED SQUARE NEBULA

SPACE JEWEL
The Red Square Nebula, a planetary nebula, looks exactly like it sounds: like a glowing red box. Inside the box is a bright white core. The edges form perfect right angles. Scientists say the Red Square Nebula is one of the most symmetrical objects ever seen in space.

Dwarfs

WHITE DWARFS

The star's remaining core becomes a white dwarf. (These dwarfs are different from those in the main sequence stage.) A white dwarf is a small star—dense, and losing much of its brightness—but very hot. Eventually, white dwarf stars cool down and fade away. They become black dwarfs, which do not release any heat or light.

THE RING NEBULA
The ring of material was once part of the star in the middle. The central star is now a white dwarf.

THAT'S ASTRONOMICAL!

White dwarfs are very dense objects. Just a single teaspoon of white dwarf matter would weigh 5.5 tons (4,990 kg)— as much as an elephant on Earth!

WEIGH COOL!

A white dwarf's gravity is about 350,000 times as strong as Earth's.

One of the most powerful and spectacular occurrences in space is the explosion of a supernova. As a supergiant star runs out of energy, its core becomes iron. Then, like a roof without beams to hold it up, the supergiant's outer layers collapse, releasing large amounts of matter into space.

SUPERNOVA REMNANTS

Almost 1,000 years ago, Chinese and Japanese astronomers recorded a violent supernova explosion that left behind an amazing impression in space: the Crab Nebula.

GALACTIC FACT

The energy from just one supernova explosion is equal to all the energy the Sun will put out in its lifetime.

STELLAR STATS
CRAB NEBULA

LOCATION
➡ Taurus constellation

AGE
➡ 1,000 years old

FIRST DISCOVERED
➡ July 4, 1054 by Far East astronomers

NOTED AND NAMED
➡ 1731, by British astronomer John Bevis; 1758, by French astronomer Charles Messier

DISTANCE FROM EARTH
➡ 6,500 light-years

SIZE
➡ 11 light-years across

ENERGY
➡ Produces 75,000 times more energy than the Sun

CRAB NEBULA

KEPLER'S SUPERNOVA

In 1604, Johannes Kepler discovered a very bright supernova in the Milky Way, later dubbed Kepler's Supernova (SN1604).

Remnant of Kepler's supernova.

EUREKA!

Amateur astronomer Caroline Moore was 14 years old when she discovered a rare supernova in the Pegasus constellation in 2008. The International Astronomical Union told Caroline she had found a very faint supernova—1,000 times dimmer than usual. Her discovery is named SN2008ha.

Kathryn Aurora Gray was 10 years old when she discovered a supernova in the Camelopardalis constellation in 2010. Her discovery is named SN2010lt.

SN2008ha

Neutron Stars

Neutrons are created when a massive star collapses and rebounds in a supernova explosion, leaving behind a highly compacted core. This core becomes a neutron star. They are very dense. How dense are they? If a neutron star were a sugar cube, that small sugar cube would weigh as much as 20 million elephants!

NEUTRON STAR FACTS

➡ A neutron star has a mass greater than 1.5 times that of the Sun.

➡ It has so much gravity, anything that came close would immediately explode.

➡ When a neutron star is formed, it rotates in space. As it rotates, it compresses, pulling in on itself, and spins even faster.

➡ The fastest-spinning neutron star ever discovered rotated at a rate of 716 times per second.

PULSAR FACTS

➡ Pulsars (short for pulsating radio stars) are fast spinning neutron stars that release energy pulses.

➡ They emit radiation and light that shine rhythmically. Some call pulsars "zosmic Lighthouses."

➡ To date, 650 pulsars have been discovered, but astronomers believe there may be at least 10,000 active in the Milky Way.

MAGNETAR FACTS

➡ Magnetars are neutron stars that release a steady glow of X-rays and have a powerful magnetic field.

➡ These magnetic fields are about 1,000 trillion times as strong as Earth's magnetic field.

➡ A magnetar's magnetic field disappears within 10,000 years.

➡ If a magnetar were only 100,000 miles (160,000 km) away from Earth, it would wipe out all the electronic data in the world.

DIGITAL RENDERING OF A MAGNETAR

Black Holes

When a very heavy star explodes, instead of becoming a neutron star, it becomes a stellar black hole. A black hole is a place where ordinary gravity has become so strong that it pulls in everything around it that reaches its event horizon—even light, the fastest thing there is, gets drawn inside. Once something crosses the event horizon, it must go inside the black hole. However, despite their power, black holes don't last forever. They evaporate slowly, eventually returning their energy to the universe.

WORD

Event horizon describes a theoretical boundary around a black hole. Nothing that crosses it can escape.

WHAT'S INSIDE A BLACK HOLE?

It's a mystery! Scientists know that black holes have a lot of mass, but no one knows exactly what the inside of a black hole looks like.

WHERE ARE BLACK HOLES CREATED?

Black holes form in places where matter gets very dense.

HOW BIG ARE THEY?

Black holes come in different sizes. Some are very large: they contain as much material as 100 million Suns and measure several million miles or kilometers across.

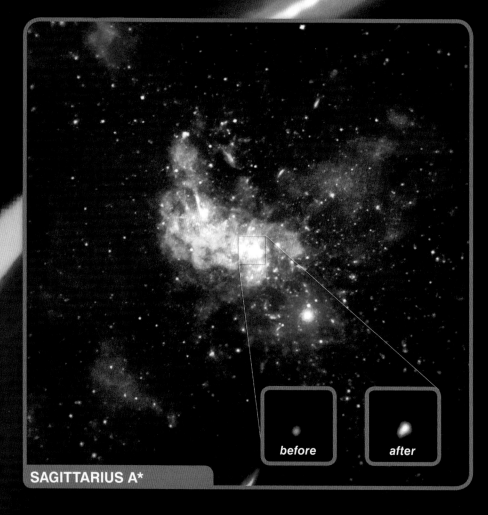

▶ There's a supermassive black hole right in the center of the Milky Way! The small images show evidence of an eruption 2 million years ago.

SAGITTARIUS A*

before

after

Black hole shredding a star

BLACK HOLE SN1979C

WHAT IF...
YOU FELL INTO
A BLACK HOLE?

If you fell inside feet first, your feet would be pulled in faster than your head—so you'd be stretched like a string of spaghetti.

GALACTIC FACT

Detected in 1970, Cygnus X-1 was the first black hole to be discovered. Scientists estimate there are hundreds of billions of black holes in the universe.

ASK HAKEEM...

COULD A BLACK HOLE SWALLOW THE ENTIRE UNIVERSE?

No, it would be impossible. The universe is far too large! The black hole in the center of the Milky Way has been there for several billion years without consuming it. And we are 30,000 light-years away from the center. So we are completely safe!

Binary (double) stars and multistar systems are two or more stars that are linked by gravity, so they orbit one another. Observing them has allowed scientists to more easily compare star behavior. Inside a multistar system, the brightest star is classified as the primary star and usually has a letter A next to it. The other stars in the system are called B, C, and so on.

TYPES OF BINARY STARS

VISUAL BINARY STARS

These are two stars far enough apart to be seen as separate objects through a telescope. They can be tough to find if one of the stars is very bright, because it often hides the second star.

SPECTROSCOPIC BINARY STARS

These stars are close together and orbit so quickly they look like one star. Astronomers find them by analyzing their spectra.

ASTROMETRIC BINARY STARS

One star can't be seen, but astronomers know there is a second star because the first star moves back and forth as it orbits the system's center of mass.

ASK HAKEEM...

COULD TWO STARS JOIN TO FORM ONE BIG STAR?

It happens all the time! Binary stars can merge to create larger stars. As the stars age, they swell up, and if they are in dense environments, they eventually merge into each other's orbits. In astronomy, a "contact binary" is a binary star system whose stars are so close that they touch.

STELLAR STATS
PROXIMA CENTAURI

DISCOVERED
➜ 1915 by Scottish astronomer Robert Innes

CLAIM TO FAME
➜ Closest star to the Sun

LOCATION
➜ Centaurus constellation

TYPE OF STAR
➜ Red dwarf star

DISTANCE
➜ 4.3 light-years away

SIZE
➜ 0.07 times the Sun's radius

BRIGHTNESS
➜ 18,000 times fainter than the Sun

CONTACT BINARY

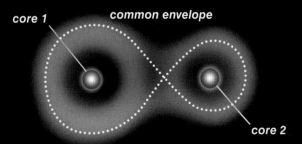

core 1

common envelope

core 2

ALPHA CENTAURI TRIPLE STAR SYSTEM

This star system near our solar system includes Alpha Centauri A, Alpha Centauri B, and Proxima Centauri. Alpha Centauri A and B are binary stars. Proxima Centauri, the third in this system, is the closest star to our Sun.

Alpha Centauri B

Proxima Centauri

Alpha Centauri A

nergy exists on Earth and in space. On Earth, electromagnetic energy is what powers things like computers and televisions. It's what lets you send text messages on a cell phone, listen to a radio, pop popcorn in the microwave, and much more. In space, the Sun and stars naturally give off energy.

Electromagnetic energy takes several different forms. There's one type that you can see on your own and many others that you cannot. Let's look at each of these, and how scientists are able to detect invisible energy in the universe.

HOW ENERGY TRAVELS

Energy travels in waves, and each type of energy has a different wavelength. This is called the electromagnetic spectrum. For example, radio waves, which carry the least amount of energy, are very long waves. Gamma rays, which carry the most energy, are very short waves.

WORD

Wavelength is the distance between two peaks of a wave.

THE ELECTROMAGNETIC SPECTRUM

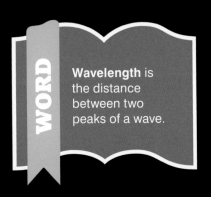

Visible Light

Infrared

Microwave

Radio

ENERGY

WAVELENGTH

VISIBLE ENERGY: LIGHT

Did you know that light is a form of energy? Everything you see with the naked eye or a telescope, from landscapes on Earth to planets in space, is because of visible light.

Visible light is in the middle of the electromagnetic spectrum. White light is really made up of colors, like you see in a rainbow after a spring rain. A fun way to remember the colors in their wavelength order is to use this acronym: ROY G. BIV.

THE VISIBLE LIGHT SPECTRUM

RED ORANGE YELLOW GREEN BLUE INDIGO VIOLET

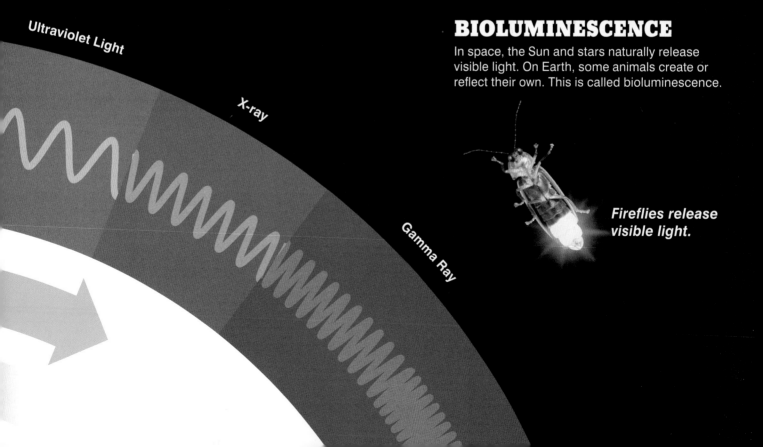

Ultraviolet Light

X-ray

Gamma Ray

BIOLUMINESCENCE

In space, the Sun and stars naturally release visible light. On Earth, some animals create or reflect their own. This is called bioluminescence.

Fireflies release visible light.

Invisible Energy

What about the other types of electromagnetic energy, the types that you can't see with the naked eye? There are invisible but powerful forms of energy out there: radio waves, microwaves, infrared waves, ultraviolet rays, X-rays, and gamma rays.

RADIO WAVES

- Radio waves range from around a foot (0.3 m) to several miles long.
- On Earth, these are often used to transmit data and have been used for radio, radar, and computer networks.
- In space, celestial objects like planets, comets and galaxies emit radio waves.

Satellite dishes use radio waves

Microwaves help radar guns track the speed of a baseball pitch or a moving car.

MICROWAVES

- Microwaves have the second-longest wavelengths. Their wavelengths are measured in centimeters.
- On Earth, we use microwaves to cook food, to transmit information, and in radar that helps predict the weather. Microwaves are useful in communication because they can get through clouds and smoke.
- In space, the Sun, galaxies, and pulsars are all sources of microwave radiation.

INFRARED WAVES

- Anything that gives off heat—including the human body!—radiates infrared waves.
- "Near" infrared waves are closer to visible light in wavelength. These are the waves used in your TV remote to change channels. Far infrared waves are farther away from visible light in wavelength. Far infrared waves release heat.
- Infrared technology helps us learn more about the origins of galaxies in space.

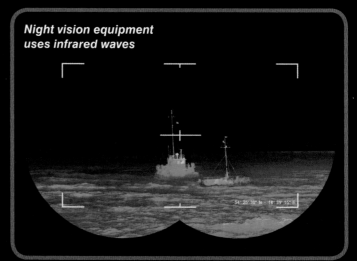
Night vision equipment uses infrared waves

ULTRAVIOLET RAYS

➡ Ultraviolet waves are shorter than infrared and visible light waves.
➡ On Earth, some insects, such as bumblebees, can see ultraviolet light.
➡ Ultraviolet rays released by the Sun can give us sunburns on Earth.
➡ In space, telescopes like the Hubble Space Telescope use ultraviolet light to see stars that are extremely far away.

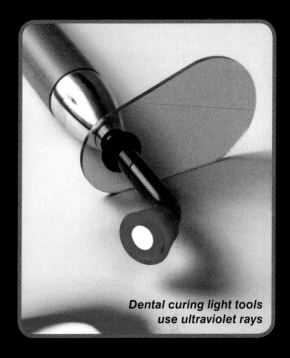

Dental curing light tools use ultraviolet rays

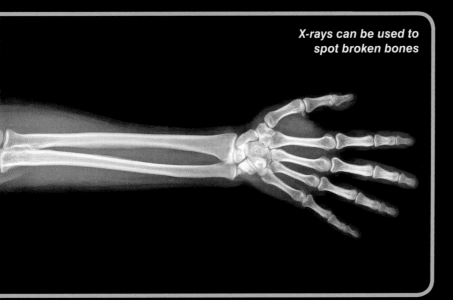

X-rays can be used to spot broken bones

X-RAYS

➡ X-rays have extremely small wavelengths.
➡ On Earth, medical professionals use X-ray technology to see inside people.
➡ Many space objects give off X-rays, including stars, some nebulas, gases, and supernova remnants.

GAMMA RAYS

➡ Gamma rays are the very shortest waves and have more energy than any other wave.
➡ On Earth, they are produced in high-energy nuclear explosions.
➡ In space, the hottest objects, like supernovas, release gamma rays.

Gamma rays produce nuclear explosions

If so much energy is invisible, how do scientists find it in the universe? They can't use a regular telescope, since it only detects visible light. Instead, they use special instruments that can measure the other types of energy in order to study deep space.

Telescopes that detect gamma ray, ultraviolet, or X-rays must be used from space because Earth's atmosphere prevents them from reaching the surface.

WORD

Cosmic rays are high-energy particles that live outside the Earth's atmosphere. Cosmic rays include X-rays and gamma rays.

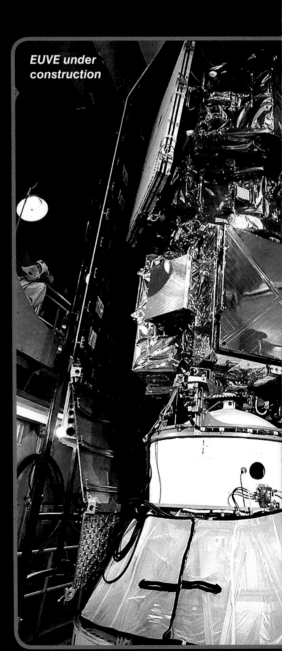

EUVE under construction

RADIO ASTRONOMY:
SQUARE KILOMETER ARRAY (SKA)

Even though there is no sound in space, objects there do give off some radio waves. Co-hosted by South Africa and Australia, the SKA will be the largest radio telescope in the world. Astronomers hope this telescope will help answer questions about dark matter and life on other planets. This telescope is so large that the computer inside it will have the processing power of 100 million PCs.

ULTRAVIOLET RAY ASTRONOMY:
EXTREME ULTRAVIOLET EXPLORER (EUVE)

By observing ultraviolet light, we have learned more about the Sun, the temperatures and the chemicals inside stars in their early stages of life, and how far away celestial objects are from Earth.

NASA's Extreme Ultraviolet Explorer satellite, a spinning spacecraft, has been exploring space for seventeen years. The EUVE has discovered a new group of white dwarf stars and has found 801 space objects.

Chandra X-ray image of Superbubble DEM L50 (composite)

X-RAY ASTRONOMY:
CHANDRA X-RAY OBSERVATORY

The Chandra X-ray Observatory is the world's most powerful X-ray telescope. It is in orbit above Earth's atmosphere so that it can detect exploding stars, galaxy clusters, and black holes. In fact, in April 2015, Chandra found a group of unusual giant black holes that have been gobbling up matter in space.

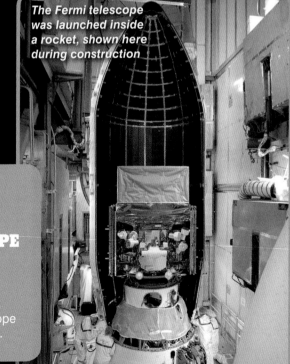

The Fermi telescope was launched inside a rocket, shown here during construction

GAMMA RAY ASTRONOMY:
FERMI GAMMA RAY TELESCOPE

Gamma ray telescopes search for bursts of these rays to help astronomers find things like supernovas and pulsars. This new gamma ray telescope was launched June 11, 2008. Fermi carries two instruments, the Large Area Telescope (LAT) and the Gamma-ray Burst Monitor (GBM).

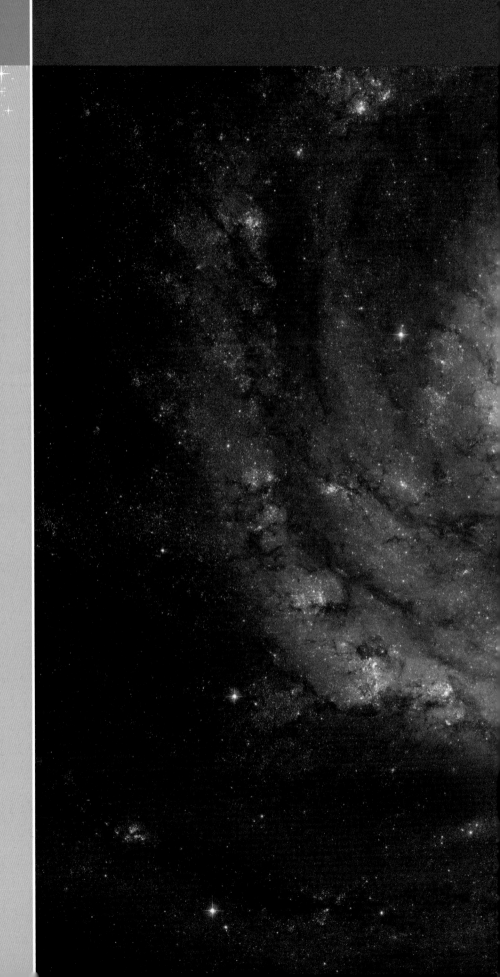

AT A GLANCE

GALAXIES

➡ A galaxy's shape can be spiral, barred spiral, elliptical, or irregular.

➡ Our solar system's galaxy is called the Milky Way.

➡ The Local Group includes the Milky Way and more than 50 other galaxies.

➡ The Magellanic Clouds are dwarf galaxies that orbit the Milky Way.

➡ Galaxy Clusters are the largest objects in the universe held together by gravity.

➡ Quasars: the most distant observable objects in the universe.

MYSTERIES OF SPACE

➡ How has the universe evolved since it was formed?

➡ Is the the universe expanding?

➡ What is the future of the universe?

THE HUBBLE TELESCOPE

➡ This orbiting telescope has captured amazing photos of objects in space.

➡ It provides scientists with valuable information.

The Universe Beyond

The universe is everything around us—Earth and everything in space beyond it. It's gigantic, and even with the amazing Hubble Space Telescope, which observes and photographs space, we have seen only a tiny part of it. The universe has not always been the same size. In fact, it has been growing larger at high speed.

What Is a Galaxy?

Galaxies are enormous collections of stars, dust, and interstellar gas—all held together by gravity. A single galaxy can contain hundreds of billions of stars, and it's estimated that there are more than 170 billion galaxies packed into the observable universe. Our Solar System is in the galaxy known as the Milky Way.

ANATOMY OF A SPIRAL GALAXY

A spiral or barred spiral galaxy, like the Milky Way, contains different parts.

BULGE
The bulge is in the middle of the galaxy. This part is round and is made up mostly of old stars, gas, and dust.

DISK
The area around the bulge is flat like a pancake. This area includes many young stars, and some old stars.

SPIRAL GALAXY
This kind of galaxy has a large bulge in the center, a flat disk, and spiral arms that create new stars.

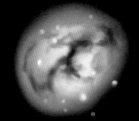

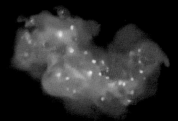

BARRED SPIRAL GALAXY
This is a spiral galaxy that has a bar-shaped group of stars in the center.

ELLIPTICAL GALAXY
This type of galaxy appears oval-shaped, with no disk or arms. Elliptical galaxies contain very old stars and don't actively create new ones.

IRREGULAR GALAXY
Irregular galaxies are not spiral or elliptical, but many used to be one or the other. There are also small ones called dwarf irregular galaxies. Astronomers believe that a galaxy becomes irregular when it has some kind of accident that changes its shape. These galaxies contain new stars.

GALLERY OF GALAXIES

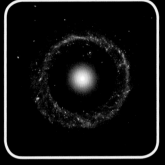

Hoag's Object Galaxy

Black Eye Galaxy

Bode's Galaxy

Tadpole Galaxy

Cigar Galaxy

NGC 1300 Galaxy

Coma Cluster Galaxy

NGC 1672 Galaxy

NGC 3314a&b Galaxies

Spindle Galaxy

Sombrero Galaxy　　*Triplet Arp 274 Galaxies*

ASK HAKEEM...

HAVE YOU EVER DISCOVERED A GALAXY?

Claiming galaxies for our own is not really what we scientists do. When scientists examine the night sky, they are always in search of new celestial objects, but it is usually a team effort. Not too long ago, I coauthored a paper on recent discoveries of satellite dwarf galaxies, and that was pretty exciting!

You are here—our solar system lives in a galaxy called the Milky Way. Until 1924, it was the only known galaxy. It looks just like a sparkly whirlpool, with four large spiral arms, plus two smaller arms, that look like they are hugging the center. Brand-new stars are constantly born inside the arms. The solar system is located in the arm known as the Orion Arm.

STELLAR STATS
MILKY WAY GALAXY

CATEGORY
➡ Barred spiral galaxy

NUMBER OF STARS
➡ 200–400 billion

MASS
➡ 400–800 billion times that of the Sun

DIAMETER
➡ 150,000 light-years

AGE
➡ 13.2 billion years old

DOES THE MILKY WAY MOVE?

Absolutely! The Milky Way is constantly rotating. Its arms are moving through space—and our solar system travels with them—at 515,000 miles per hour (828,812 km).

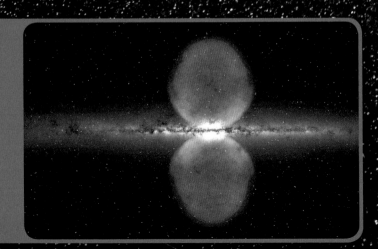

NASA's *Fermi* telescope discovered giant gas bubbles that extend from the center of the Milky Way in 2010. They are expanding at a rapid rate, and now extend 30,000 light-years in either direction (mapped in this artist's conception).

HOW DID THE MILKY WAY GET ITS NAME?

The ancient Romans named it Via Lactea, which means "road of milk," because it looks like a trail of spilled milk in the sky.

CAN YOU SEE THE MILKY WAY?

Yes! As long as you are viewing Earth's night sky from a dark place, the Milky Way is visible. It looks like a fuzzy band that stretches from horizon to horizon. When you see it in the sky, you are looking at the galaxy on its side, since we are inside it.

An infrared image of the Milky Way taken by the Spitzer Space Telescope

Close-up of the Milky Way

The Galactic Core

It's one of the most haunting parts of the Milky Way. It's stormy, with hot gases and monstrous magnetic fields. It's huge, has a massive gravitational pull, and is crammed full of stars. It's the galactic core—the center of our galaxy—27,000 light-years from Earth.

The galactic core contains the most stars in the Milky Way. Many of the stars inside it are among the oldest in the galaxy. The stars here are so close together that they are only light-weeks away from one another (while stars near Earth, for example, are light-years away from one another).

The assembly of the Spitzer space telescope

CAN WE SEE IT?

As bright as it is in the galactic core, it's very hard for scientists to see. Earth lives way out in the disk of the Milky Way—a disk filled to the brim with clouds and dust that form a kind of starry fog. It wasn't until the 20th century that astronomers directly observed it, with the help of infrared telescopes. In infrared light, the fog vanishes and the bright center is revealed.

Main image shows the center of the Milky Way (Spitzer Space telescope image)

Bright star cluster Messier 7, visible to the naked eye (near Scorpius constellation)

THAT'S ASTRONOMICAL!

The Sun takes 240 million years to make one revolution around the galactic core. This is known as a galactic year.

Black hole close-up

THE HUNT FOR A BLACK HOLE

Astronomers suspect that most galaxies, including the Milky Way, have giant black holes in their cores. The tricky part is that they are hidden. So astronomers look for unusual star behavior or increased emissions of light that could be caused by black holes. It's like watching a detective show—there are lots of clues.

The first sign that there may be a black hole in the center of the Milky Way came in 1974. Astronomers detected strong radio emissions coming from an area of the galactic core named Sagittarius A. It seemed to the astronomers that there must be a disk of material orbiting around something—an unseen object!

Then, in 1995, astronomers used infrared telescopes to examine some individual stars inside Sagittarius A. These stars were faster than most. They were racing around, shifting positions, and orbiting something invisible.

Astronomers could tell the stars were orbiting an object small in size. But the timing and speed of the orbits suggested that the object's mass had to be enormous. A black hole fits that profile.

The Local Group

Buckle up! We are traveling far beyond our galaxy. The Milky Way is part of a larger interstellar neighborhood of more than 50 galaxies called the Local Group. This is deep space, where there are trillions of stars and planets, and some unidentified happenings. The most massive galaxies in the Local Group are the Andromeda Galaxy, the Milky Way, and the Triangulum Galaxy.

GALACTIC FACT

The Local Group measures about 10 million light-years across.

STELLAR STATS

ANDROMEDA GALAXY (M31)

CATEGORY
➡ Spiral galaxy

DISTANCE FROM THE MILKY WAY
➡ 2.5 million light-years

NUMBER OF STARS
➡ 1 trillion

MASS
➡ 1 trillion times that of the Sun

DIAMETER
➡ 260,000 light-years

AGE
➡ 10 billion years old

THE ANDROMEDA GALAXY

Formerly known as the Great Andromeda Nebula, the Andromeda Galaxy is our closest neighboring galaxy. And it's huge—more than twice the size of the Milky Way. It can be seen from Earth's Northern Hemisphere even without a telescope. Andromeda and the Milky Way are racing toward each other, 100 times faster than a speeding bullet. But don't worry! It will take 4 billion years for them to meet.

EUREKA!

In 1925, Edwin Hubble found many stars in the area now known as the Andromeda Galaxy. Hubble figured out that the stars there weren't in the Milky Way and instead were ten times farther away. This discovery was made possible by the earlier work of astronomer Henrietta Leavitt, who discovered how to figure out a star's luminosity (brightness) and therefore how far away it is.

THE TRIANGULUM GALAXY

Also known as the Pinwheel Galaxy (also the name of another galaxy), this is the third-largest galaxy in the Local Group. Barely visible in Earth's night sky, this faraway galaxy has two cool features. First, its clouds are fluorescent and infused with ultraviolet light. Second, these clouds are creating so many young stars that if this galaxy were closer to Earth, it would be the brightest light in the sky.

STELLAR STATS
TRIANGULUM GALAXY (M33)

CATEGORY
➡ Spiral galaxy

DISTANCE FROM MILKY WAY
➡ 3 million light-years

NUMBER OF STARS
➡ 40 billion

MASS
➡ 10–40 billion times that of the Sun

DIAMETER
➡ 60,000 light-years

AGE
➡ 13.2 billion years old

Milky Way

LMC
SMC

M31 (Andromeda)

M33 (Triangulum)

The Magellanic Clouds

Astronomers have discovered that our galaxy has an amazing feature: In the past, it has gobbled up several smaller galaxies, thanks to its gravitational pull. Currently, two nearby dwarf galaxies—the Large and Small Magellanic Clouds—are orbiting the Milky Way.

THE LARGE AND SMALL MAGELLANIC CLOUDS

These galaxies are visible in the night sky from Earth's Southern Hemisphere. The Small Magellanic Cloud is one of the most distant objects that can be seen with the naked eye. A bridge of gas, called the Magellanic Stream, connects the two clouds. Scientists have observed stars forming in this area.

NEW INTEL

The Spitzer Space Telescope recently snapped a bright picture of the Large Magellanic Cloud. Using infrared light, astronomers can study the life cycle of stars. In this image, older stars are represented by blue light, and new stars and clouds are represented by red light.

STELLAR STATS

LARGE MAGELLANIC CLOUD

NICKNAME
➡ LMC

CATEGORY
➡ Dwarf irregular galaxy

MASS
➡ 10 billion times that of the Sun

DIAMETER
➡ 14,000 light-years

AGE
➡ Approximately 1.6 billion years old

LARGE MAGELLANIC CLOUD

Main image shows Large Megallanic Cloud

GALACTIC FACT

The LMC has been classified as a dwarf irregular galaxy, but recent discoveries of a bar and portion of a spiral arm suggest it may be a "disrupted spiral galaxy" due to gravitational interactions with the Milky Way.

SMALL MAGELLANIC CLOUD

STELLAR STATS

SMALL MAGELLANIC CLOUD

NICKNAME
➡ SMC

CATEGORY
➡ Dwarf irregular galaxy

MASS
➡ 6.5 billion times that of the Sun

DIAMETER
➡ 7,000 light-years

AGE
➡ Approximately 1.6 billion years old

DID YOU KNOW?

The Magellanic Clouds are named after the famous 16th-century explorer Ferdinand Magellan, whose ship was the first to travel all the way around the globe.

Galaxy Clusters

No one knows exactly how galaxy clusters—multiple galaxies bound together by gravity—are created. In a cluster, the galaxies all orbit one another. The giant galaxy cluster Abell 2744 has been nicknamed Pandora's Cluster for all the different things found inside.

GALACTIC FACT

Galaxy clusters are the largest objects in the universe held together by gravity.

PANDORA'S CLUSTER

Astronomers have studied Pandora with many kinds of telescopes—ones on Earth and in space. They've learned that Pandora has a mass that's about 400 trillion times that of the Sun. It is thought to be the result of several galaxy clusters colliding, forming an even bigger cluster.

STELLAR STATS
ABELL 2744

NICKNAME
➡ Pandora's Cluster

DESCRIPTION
➡ Giant galaxy cluster

LOCATION
➡ Sculptor constellation, in the Southern Hemisphere

DISTANCE FROM EARTH
➡ 3.5–4 billion light-years

AGE
➡ 350 million years old

SIZE
➡ 2 million light-years across

DISCOVERED
➡ 1958, by American astronomer George Ogden Abell

ABELL 2744

▶Close-up of Abell 2744's center showing dark matter

COSMIC COLLISIONS

When two galaxies are close together, they don't move away from each other as they would normally. Instead, their gravity pulls them toward each other. As they move closer, the attraction gets stronger, until they sloooowly crash into each other—this may take at least half a billion years. Then what happens?

➡ Many stars pass by one another since they are so far apart. Some stars are flung out of orbit.

➡ Huge clouds and millions of stars are pushed together, and new stars may be born.

➡ Eventually the galaxy settles into its new shape, although this may take 2 billion years.

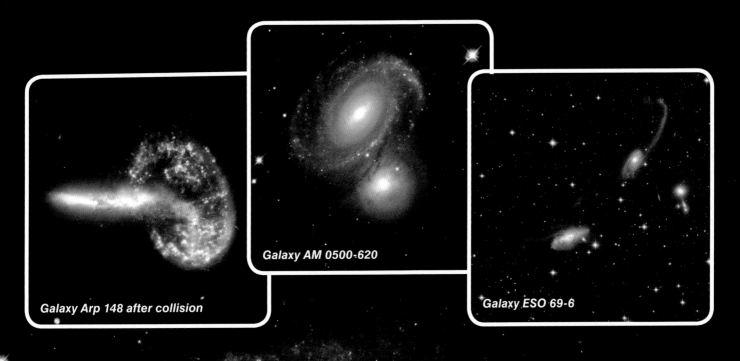

Galaxy AM 0500-620

Galaxy Arp 148 after collision

Galaxy ESO 69-6

◀Galaxies NGC 2207 and IC 2163 collide

Sometimes, matter spiraling into a black hole is torn apart and glows so intensely that it creates the brightest objects in the universe—quasars. Like many space objects, quasars give off enormous amounts of energy. Did you know that they shine a trillion times brighter than the Sun? Because quasars are so bright, they drown out the light from other stars in their galaxies.

WORD

Quasar is actually short for *quasi-stellar radio source*. Quasars are the most energetic known objects in the universe.

◄ *ULAS J1120+0641, the most distant quasar found so far.*

WHAT ARE QUASARS?

A quasar is an extremely bright spot near the edge of a supermassive black hole. Scientists think that black holes are the engines that power quasars. Quasars are the farthest observable objects from our galaxy.

HOW OLD ARE THEY?

Quasars are very old—at least several billion years old. In fact, quasars in particular offer clues to the age of the universe. The light of a quasar that is 5 billion light-years away takes 5 billion years to get to Earth. Since Earth is 4.6 billion years old, we see the quasar as it was before Earth was born.

QUASAR HE 1013-2136 WITH TIDAL TAILS

Supermassive black hole NGC 4258

Black hole

WHITE HOLES

Are there white holes in the universe? They have yet to be detected, but experts think it's possible. In theory, white holes would be the opposite of black holes. A black hole pulls matter into it, whereas a white hole would spew out material. A black hole has a one-way entrance, and a white hole would be exit only.

QUASAR IN AN ELLIPTICAL GALAXY

Origins of the Universe

The universe formed 13.8 billion years ago. As it expanded over billions of years, gravity caused some matter to clump and become more complex structures—planets, stars, and galaxies. It contains billions of galaxies, each containing billions of stars. The space between stars and galaxies appears empty. But even those places contain space dust, light and heat, magnetic fields, and cosmic rays.

How big is the universe? Even the most experienced scientists don't yet know the full size of the universe, because no one has found its edges. All we know is the observable universe—what we can see with the help of telescopes—and it is about 93 billion light-years across.

DID YOU KNOW?

When a radio isn't properly tuned to a station, you hear static. About 1 percent of that noise is radiation left over from the Big Bang. Astronomers call it the cosmic microwave background.

▼ All-sky image of cosmic microwave background, showing the universe 13.77 billion years ago.

LOOKING BACK IN TIME

Since galaxies and other distant objects are light-years away, when we use telescopes to view them, we are actually seeing them as they were in the past. Remember, we can't see a distant object until its light travels through space and reaches us on Earth. So if you are viewing a galaxy that is 2 million light-years away, you are actually seeing it as it was 2 million years ago. In a sense, telescopes are our time machines.

COSMIC TIMELINE: IN WITH A BANG

◀ The Big Bang

10^{-43} sec	10^{-32} sec	3 min	300,000 years	1 billion years	15 billion years	Today

The Big Bang theory says that the universe was once much smaller, hotter, and denser than it is now—its mass was packed into a region smaller than a basketball. When the Big Bang occurred 13.8 billion years ago, space, time, matter, and energy were born. Space everywhere expanded. As the universe began to cool off, the material inside began to form objects. After the Big Bang, gravity brought some of the matter together, and planets and stars began to develop.

The Expanding Universe

Your world is getting bigger all the time. Moments after the Big Bang happened, the universe began to expand—and it's still growing, even today. The Big Bang theory is how most scientists agree the universe began. What evidence supports this idea?

SCIENTIFIC EVIDENCE OF THE BIG BANG

Observations of what's going on in space right now support the theory of how the universe started.

1. EXPANSION OF THE UNIVERSE

➡ **Fact:** Every galaxy in the universe, except the very closest ones, is moving away from us. The rate at which a galaxy is moving away is directly related to how far away it is.

➡ **Meaning:** Because this is true across the board, it suggests the whole universe is expanding. Objects in the universe (like galaxies, stars, planets, you) are not expanding, but it is the space between galaxies that is expanding. As the universe expands, it cools. This means that in the past the universe was smaller and hotter.

2. HYDROGEN-HELIUM RATIO

➡ **Fact:** Everywhere we look in the universe, the ratio of the elements hydrogen to helium is about the same. But this is surprising. Scientists wouldn't expect this to be true because stars convert hydrogen to helium, so the ratio should change from place to place.

➡ **Meaning:** Some process must have occurred everywhere in the universe to cook some (but not all) of the hydrogen into helium. So everywhere in the universe must once have been as hot as the center of a star. A lot of light also must have been present to prevent all of the hydrogen from cooking into helium. Finally, this must have occurred within the first 15 minutes of the universe's existence, or else there would be very few neutrons in the universe today.

3. COSMIC MICROWAVE BACKGROUND

➡ **Fact:** Scientists have measured a background of microwaves that fills all of space.

➡ **Meaning:** This is the light that was present during the first 15 minutes of the universe. Study of this light has indicated conclusively that the universe was once much smaller, hotter, and denser, and that the universe is 13.8 billion years old.

TRY THIS

Take an uninflated balloon and tape several coins to it. Imagine the balloon is the universe and each coin is a galaxy. Now, blow up the balloon. What can you observe?

When you put air in the balloon, the coins all move away from one another, but they do not change size. Similarly, as the universe expands, galaxies retain their size and are generally moving away from one another. (Exceptions occur when galaxies are very close together and the strength of their gravity causes them to collide.)

IT'S GETTING FASTER

It was once thought that the universe would grow at the same rate forever. But the universe is doing something different—its rate of expansion is speeding up.

The Fate of the Universe

There are many ideas about how the universe may end someday. But none of them looks like a Hollywood movie about the end of the world. No one is predicting an alien invasion or a massive flood. Instead, researchers have different scientific theories on how the universe might evolve over the next few billion years. And they involve a force that we can't see but for which there is evidence in the universe—dark energy.

DARK MATTER AND DARK ENERGY

Dark matter is material that does not emit, absorb, or scatter light. But scientists know it exists because of how it affects visible matter like stars and galaxies.

Dark energy is a force that exists in empty space. It got its name because it cannot be detected with any kind of instrument scientists have today. However, based on unusual behavior of some objects in space, scientists think it may be causing space to expand.

DARK MATTER
➡ Dark matter attracts, pulling things into it.
➡ Dark matter clumps because of gravity, like normal matter does.
➡ Dark matter affects galaxies.

DARK ENERGY
➡ Dark energy repels, pushing things away.
➡ Dark energy does not clump because of gravity.
➡ Dark energy affects a very large volume of space.

COMPOSITION OF THE UNIVERSE

Dark Energy: 68 %

Dark Matter: 27 %

Normal Matter: 5 % —its rate of expansion is speeding up.

Deep space

WHAT WILL HAPPEN TO THE UNIVERSE?

There are different theories about how the universe will change in the future. Here are three that scientists are studying.

1. THE BIG RIP THEORY

Every galaxy in the universe, except the very closest ones, is moving away from us. The rate at which a galaxy is moving away is directly related to how far away it is.

2. THE BIG CRUNCH THEORY

The universe may stop expanding at some point in time. And when it does, it will collapse into itself, pulling everything into it until it turns into a supermassive black hole. The problem with this theory is that astronomers can see that dark energy is still expanding the universe, so there's very little chance we will be crunched into a black hole.

3. INDEFINITE EXPANSION THEORY

Known as Indefinite Expansion, this theory proposes that the universe will continue to expand, but at a slower rate, so it won't rip apart. Instead, it will eventually become cold, dark, and lifeless. There will be nothing in Earth's night sky, because everything will be so far away that light won't reach it.

The Hubble Space Telescope

Since 1990, the Hubble Space Telescope has been our eyes in the universe. Orbiting 340 miles (547 km) above Earth, it takes pictures of space objects and has delivered some of the most fantastic images ever captured. Hubble is one of the most successful science missions and has shed new light on the many mysteries of space.

GALACTIC FACT

The Hubble Space Telescope orbits the Earth quickly—once every 97 minutes. It would take Hubble only 10 minutes to travel across the United States.

Hubble collects light—more light than our eyes ever could. And the more light a space telescope takes in, the better the pictures it can take. As Hubble moves, its giant mirrors capture and feed light into several different optic instruments inside the telescope. These instruments gather data and send it back to scientists on Earth.

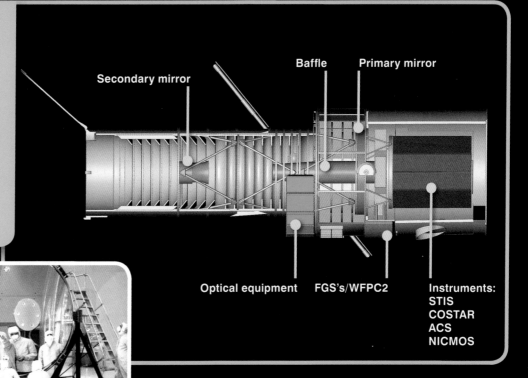

Secondary mirror

Baffle   Primary mirror

Optical equipment   FGS's/WFPC2   **Instruments:
STIS
COSTAR
ACS
NICMOS**

▶**The primary mirror is 94.5 inches (2.4 m) in diameter and weighs 1,825 pounds (828 kg).**

HUBBLE PROBES THE EARLY UNIVERSE

The Hubble telescope has revealed deeper, older areas of our universe over its 25 years photographing space. Here's a look at how our ability to see into our universe's past has increased.

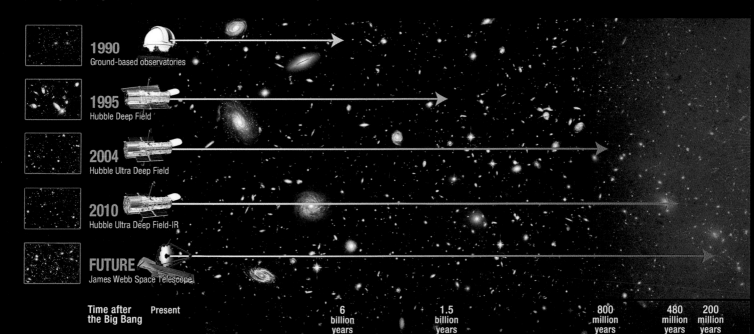

1990
Ground-based observatories

1995
Hubble Deep Field

2004
Hubble Ultra Deep Field

2010
Hubble Ultra Deep Field-IR

FUTURE
James Webb Space Telescope

| Time after the Big Bang | Present | | 6 billion years | 1.5 billion years | | 800 million years | 480 million years | 200 million years |

Hubble Discoveries

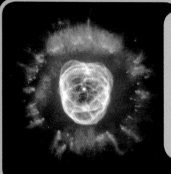

ESKIMO NEBULA

This planetary nebula was named for its resemblance to a person's head surrounded by a parka hood. It is the glowing remnant of a dying star.

WESTERLUND 2

This giant young star cluster shines with the light of more than 3,000 stars.

WR 25 (WOLF-RAYET STAR) AND TR16-244 (IN TRUMPLER 16 CLUSTER)

Located inside a cloud of gas in the Carina nebula, WR 25 is the brightest star, and Tr16-244 is the third brightest, to the upper left of WR 25.

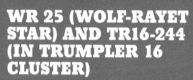

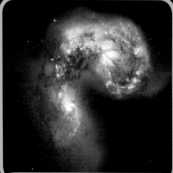

STAR CLUSTER NGC 3603

Located in the Milky Way and just about 1 million years old, this cluster has hot blue stars at its center.

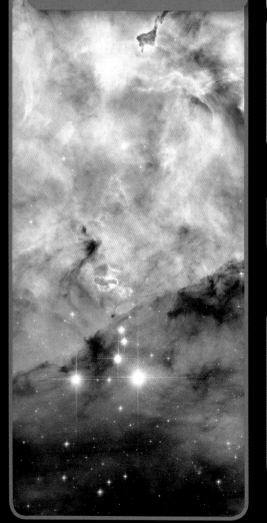

ANTENNAE GALAXIES

These spiral galaxies have been interacting with one another for a few hundred million years. Stars ripped from each galaxy form an arc between the galaxies.

BUTTERFLY NEBULA

Also known as NGC 6302, this shows gas released by a dying star.

RED SPIDER NEBULA

This planetary nebula houses one of the hottest white dwarf stars known and has gusting winds and supersonic shocks.

ECLECTIC MIX OF GALAXIES

A galaxy-rich area shows a yellow spiral galaxy, a blue galaxy of young, hot stars, and several red galaxies containing older, cooler stars.

LMC N 49

The wisps around this supernova remnant within the Large Magellanic Cloud are sheets from a stellar explosion in a neighboring galaxy.

LIGHT ECHO

Interstellar dust surrounds supergiant star V838 Monocerotis.

SATURN AND MOONS

Four of Saturn's moons are captured in this image: Enceladus, Dione, Mimas, and Titan.

TARANTULA NEBULA

This spider-shaped nebula is full of star clusters, glowing gas, and thick, dark dust. There are more than 800,000 stars and protostars within this nebula.

JUPITER TRIPLE ECLIPSE

Three of Jupiter's moons cast their shadows on Jupiter in a rare triple eclipse. From the left: Ganymede, Io, and Calisto.

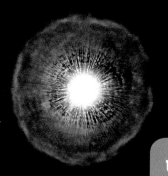

U CAMELOPARDALIS

U Cam is a red giant star surrounded by a shell of gas.

AT A GLANCE

NASA

➡ This agency studies aeronautics, exploration, science, and space technology.

➡ It has also created inventions that we use here on Earth.

MARS

➡ Plans for Mars exploration in 2020 are out of this world!

LIFE BEYOND EARTH

➡ The Kepler spacecraft has discovered more than 2,000 possible exoplanets.

➡ The oldest exoplanet is 13 billion years old.

➡ NASA is getting closer to finding more Earthlike planets.

THE FUTURE OF SPACE EXPLORATION

➡ The Transiting Exoplanet Survey Satellite (TESS) will look for planets around nearby stars.

➡ The James Webb Space Telescope will see farther into space.

➡ The Solar Probe Plus will travel to the Sun's atmosphere.

➡ Astronauts may land on an asteroid in just 10 years.

Space Exploration

The dream of leaving Earth and sending spacecraft to the Moon and other planets has come true. But although we've made fantastic achievements, there are still many more secrets of space to explore.

NASA and other space agencies are gearing up for some big new endeavors. Spacecraft will take astronauts and robotic rovers to new places. In the next 15 years, humans may be able to explore Mars.

NASA

In 1958, the U.S. Congress created the National Aeronautics and Space Administration (NASA), an agency that would coordinate America's activities in outer space. Today, NASA is based in Washington, D.C., and has locations across the country—including research centers, flight centers, space centers, test facilities, and a jet propulsion lab. You can even visit them yourself!

NASA'S VISION

"To reach for new heights and reveal the unknown so that what we do and learn will benefit all humankind."

Although it's not every day that NASA launches a new spacecraft, they study our world and the universe on a daily basis. In addition to coordinating experiments on the International Space Station and collecting data from current space missions, they are constantly working on innovations in flight, engineering, robotics, and space technologies, as well as planning future missions. And sometimes their inventions can be used right here at home.

STUDYING SPACE For more than half a century, NASA has sponsored thousands of space expeditions and has given us important information about our solar system and universe. From the Moon landing to the space shuttle program, from the Hubble Space Telescope to the International Space Station, NASA's technology and innovations have given us a better understanding of our universe.

STUDYING EARTH NASA's scientists are tracking what's going on in our environment, like changes in ocean temperature and rainfall, in order to study how climate change will affect the planet.

STUDYING THE SUN Several upcoming missions will study the Sun and the solar system, giving scientists answers to questions about the birth of the Sun and planets as well as their evolution over time.

DO YOU WANT TO WORK FOR NASA?

Science is a pretty cool gig! Have you ever thought that one day you might work for NASA? The agency needs more than just astronauts. NASA needs workers who have different skills, like engineers, mathematicians, accountants, historians, computer technicians, educators, physicians—and more. The most important thing for preparing to find a job at NASA is that you study what you like and work hard to achieve your goals.

COOL INVENTIONS FOR EARTH

NASA scientists may spend most of their time looking at the stars, but some of their inventions and innovations are used on Earth, too.

WATER FILTERS Scientists at NASA invented these when they wanted clean water in space. In order to keep water clean for longer periods of time, they placed charcoal inside water filters.

ARTIFICIAL LIMBS NASA's innovations in robotics are helping manufacturers create new and better solutions for human prosthetics.

CAMERA PHONES A NASA scientist developed the technology that now enables cell phone cameras and other imaging devices.

SHOCK-ABSORBING HELMETS No professional football player would go on the field without one. Based on NASA technology, temper foam is used in knee pads, helmets, shoulder pads, and shin guards.

INSULIN PUMPS An astronaut's health has to be monitored carefully, so the Goddard Space Flight Center developed a device that monitors a person's blood sugar levels and gives them insulin when they need it. This is now used by people with diabetes to replace painful and inconvenient insulin injections.

ARTERIOVISION NASA develops advanced imaging technology to explore our solar system, and the same technology can be used to explore our bodies. Arteriovision allows doctors to look closely at a patient's arteries and diagnose diseases.

COCHLEAR IMPLANTS A NASA engineer with poor hearing developed a surgically implantable device that allows people with little or no function in their ears to hear again, basing his work on existing NASA sensors designed to hear sounds far away in space.

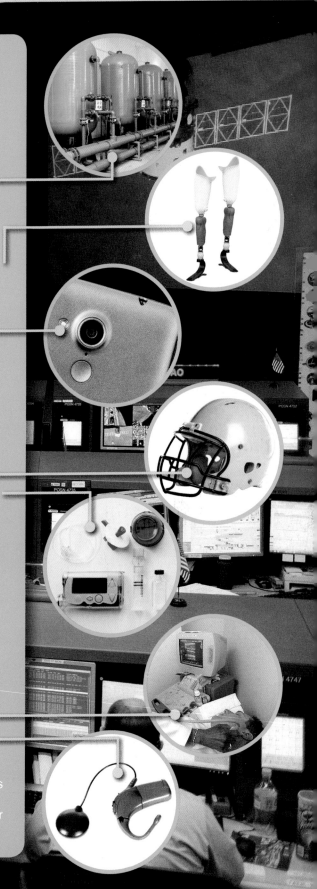

Blast Off to Mars!

Robotic explorers have visited Mars for over 30 years. Now NASA is set to pave the way for human exploration of Mars. Here are several new missions to the planet that are scheduled for the coming years and decades, and a sneak peek at the technology being developed.

THE EXOMARS PROGRAM

The European Space Agency has planned a series of missions to understand if life ever existed on Mars. Both the Russian Federal Space Agency and NASA will also participate. The ExoMars 2018 mission will land a rover on the surface of Mars, complete with instruments that will be able to tap into the interior of the Red Planet.

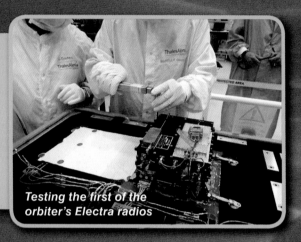

Testing the first of the orbiter's Electra radios

Hall thruster

2020 ROVER MISSION

Building on the success of the Mars rover Curiosity, the 2020 rover mission is a new, long-term mission of robotic exploration. It will look for signs of past life on Mars, collect soil samples, and test technology for future human exploration of Mars.

Ground tests have been performed to help launch new rockets to Mars

NASA'S JOURNEY TO MARS MISSION

In this groundbreaking new mission, NASA is creating technology to send humans to Mars in the 2030s. Because Mars and Earth are similar, scientists think Mars may once have had life. So it's important for scientists to study Mars's history. From it, they may be able to see what the future of Earth holds.

ASK HAKEEM...

WILL IT EVER BE POSSIBLE FOR PEOPLE TO LIVE ON MARS?

Yes! Preliminary data looks promising! It is expected that astronauts may soon be able to walk on Mars—we believe by 2035. But, because of Mars's thin atmosphere, NASA must first figure out how to protect astronauts from the radiation given off by the Sun.

Endurance Crater on Mars

Most everyone has wondered if there could be alien life on other planets. Are there more planets like Earth out in space? Well, NASA has made it a mission to find out the answers to these questions—and more.

EXOPLANETS

Featuring everything from extreme temperatures to poisonous atmospheres, the other planets in our Solar System don't seem able to support life. But there may be 160 billion other planets in the Milky Way Galaxy. These are called exoplanets, and it's possible that one or more could be Earthlike.

▲ **Kepler-452b**
July 2015

▼ **Kepler-20e**
December 2011

▼ **Kepler-186f**
April 2014

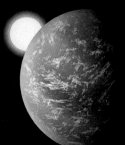

▲ **Kepler-22b**
December 2011

THE KEPLER MISSION

In March 2009, NASA launched the Kepler mission to look specifically for exoplanets that could be hospitable to life. In just the first 16 months, Kepler discovered 2,326 possible planets. The mission has been so successful that NASA has extended it to 2016.

Which planets have the best chances of supporting life? Kepler's telescope has discovered eight that are similar in size to Earth and that orbit stars that are about as far from them as the Sun is from Earth. In 2015, the Kepler mission discovered exoplanet Kepler-452b, Earth's bigger, older cousin.

FINDING EXOPLANETS

Scientists find these alien planets using the transit method, in which they look for "dips" in the brightness of a star. When there are three dips in brightness, scientists know that an exoplanet is passing across the star.

TESS

Launching in 2017, the Transiting Exoplanet Survey Satellite (TESS) is a new planet-finding mission. Scientists hope TESS will detect small planets that have bright host stars, so that they can see details of the exoplanets and their atmospheres. The plan is for TESS to monitor the brightnesses of more than 500,000 stars in two years.

THE PUFFY EXOPLANET

Exoplanet TrES-4 is 1.7 times the size of Jupiter. Scientists call it a "puffy" planet because it has a very low density, meaning it's big but lightweight.

AN EXOPLANET FAR, FAR AWAY

Exoplanet OGLE-05-390Lb is a whopping 21,000 light-years away. And it's a slow mover. This exoplanet takes 3,500 days to complete one orbit of its star.

THE OLDEST EXOPLANET

Exoplanet PSR B1620-26 b is nicknamed Methuselah, after the oldest person in the Bible. Astronomers believe it formed 13 billion years ago.

ASK HAKEEM...

WHAT KIND OF LIFE DO YOU THINK NASA COULD FIND ON OTHER HABITABLE PLANETS?

Mostly microscopic. Of course, under the right conditions, this microscopic life could evolve to larger, multicellular life-forms. What forms this life takes will depend on its environmental conditions. Most likely, it will be very different from Earth life.

What does the future of space exploration have in store for us? Will it include robots? Yes! Cool space suits? Probably! Discovering life on other planets? Maybe. Scientists around the globe are working on advanced technologies to explore not only the planets in the solar system, but also deep space. Here are some of the ways scientists hope to learn more about exoplanets, asteroids, and how stars are born and evolve.

JUNO

Traveling at 20 miles (32 km) per second, Juno is on a mission to visit Jupiter. Juno will study Jupiter's structure, giving scientists clues about its history, and will arrive in 2016.

The largest, most powerful booster built for NASA's new rocket.

NASA'S SPACE LAUNCH SYSTEM (SLS)

The power behind these heavy-duty launch rockets will propel humans deeper into space than we ever thought possible. The first SLS mission will launch a test flight—without astronauts—of the Orion spacecraft. The second SLS mission will launch Orion and a crew of four American astronauts. Target launch dates: 2018 and 2021.

SOLAR PROBE PLUS

The Solar Probe Plus mission will visit the Sun's outer atmosphere and give scientists more information about our favorite star. Target launch date: 2018.

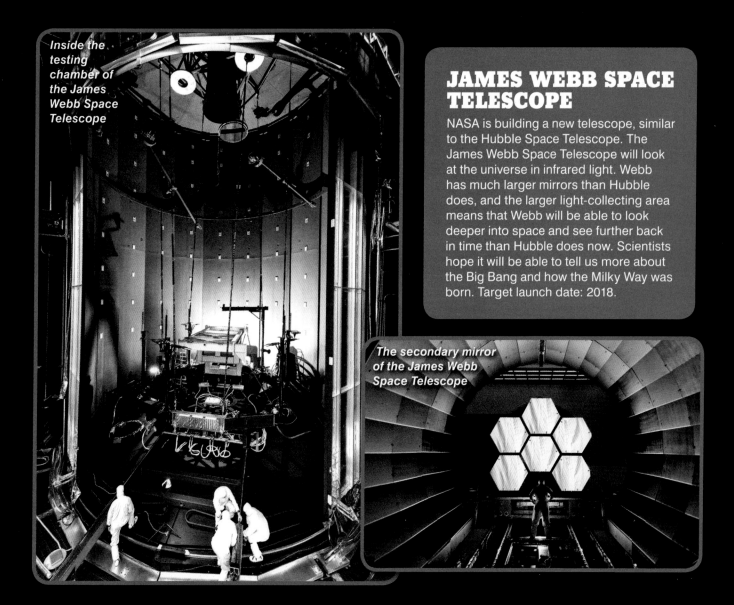

Inside the testing chamber of the James Webb Space Telescope

The secondary mirror of the James Webb Space Telescope

JAMES WEBB SPACE TELESCOPE

NASA is building a new telescope, similar to the Hubble Space Telescope. The James Webb Space Telescope will look at the universe in infrared light. Webb has much larger mirrors than Hubble does, and the larger light-collecting area means that Webb will be able to look deeper into space and see further back in time than Hubble does now. Scientists hope it will be able to tell us more about the Big Bang and how the Milky Way was born. Target launch date: 2018.

MANNED MISSION TO AN ASTEROID

In 2010, President Barack Obama announced his plans to send humans to an asteroid. Using data from OSIRIS-REx, NASA hopes to have an astronaut mission as early as 2025.

OSIRIS-REX

After traveling for three years, this mission's spacecraft will approach a 1,900-foot (579 m) asteroid named 101955 Bennu. It will use a robotic arm to take samples from the asteroid, then return to Earth in 2023. Target launch date: late 2016.

Scientists learn a lot by researching and observing. As a budding astronomer, you can start by trying these fact-finding missions.

FIND THE FACTS: PROFILE A PLANET

Choose a planet and learn all about it. Get a notebook and start researching the details of a planet. Here are some investigative questions to get you started.

➡ What does the planet look like?

➡ How big is it?

➡ How long does it take to orbit the Sun?

➡ How far is it from Earth? From the Sun?

➡ What is its atmosphere like?

➡ What is its gravity like?

➡ What is the temperature like?

➡ How many moons does it have?

➡ Are there winds on this planet?

➡ How fast do the winds move?

STUDY THE UNIVERSE: CREATE A COSMIC CALENDAR

Learning the constellations, observing the phases of the Moon, and looking for a solar eclipse or a comet are all parts of becoming a space explorer. Keeping your data and observations in a calendar will help you understand how the night sky changes over the course of a month or even a year. Each night you can write down your observations. Here's how to create your own "Cosmic Calendar." You can make your own with paper and crayons, keep notes on a smart phone or computer, or check out the space calendars (and other activities) at spaceplace.nasa.gov.

Each night, observe the sky from a dark location at the same time. (Remember, you will get the best view if you turn off the lights in and around your home.) You can use the star charts in this book, find one online, or get one at an observatory or science museum near you.

Examples of things to look for in the night sky:

➡ Can you find the Big Dipper?

➡ What other constellations can you see?

➡ Which phase of the Moon is showing?

➡ Can you find any planets in the sky?

➡ What's the brightest object in the sky?

➡ Can you find the North Star (Polaris)?

PLACES TO VISIT

CALIFORNIA

California Science Center
Los Angeles, California
californiasciencecenter.org

Includes exhibitions and hands-on activities, and the space shuttle Endeavor.

California Academy of Sciences
San Francisco, California
calacademy.org

Includes a naturalist center, a project lab, and the Morrison Planetarium.

FLORIDA

Kennedy Space Center
Titusville, Florida
kennedyspacecenter.com

Explore the history and future of American space exploration, visit the U.S. Astronaut Hall of Fame, and find out if you have "the right stuff" to be an astronaut in special interactive programs.

ILLINOIS

Adler Planetarium
Chicago, Illnois
adlerplanetarium.org

Includes ongoing and special exhibitions, three theaters, and a planetarium.

Henry Crown Space Center
Museum of Science and Industry
Chicago, Illinois
msichicago.org

Exhibits feature the "space race" from early exploration to the future of the universe.

MASSACHUSETTS

Museum of Science, Boston
Boston, Massachusetts
mos.org/planetarium

Features science and technology exhibitions, hands-on and drop-in activities, and the Charles Hayden Planetarium.

SPOT THE STATION

The International Space Station orbits Earth about every 90 minutes. That means it might be passing over your neighborhood or nearby soon. With the help of binoculars or a telescope, you can see the space station in the sky when it's overhead. Check out Spot the Station at http://spotthestation.nasa.gov to find out when it's going to be near your neighborhood, and for tips for how to spy the ISS in the sky.

NEW YORK
Rose Center for Earth and Space
American Museum of Natural History
New York, New York
amnh.org/our-research/hayden-planetarium

Includes ongoing and special exhibits, multimedia programs, and the Hayden Planetarium.

OHIO
Center of Science and Industry
Columbus, Ohio
cosi.org

Features hands-on activities and the COSI Planetarium.

WASHINGTON, D.C.
Smithsonian National Museum of Natural History
Washington, D.C.
airandspace.si.edu

Aviation and space artifacts, including the Apollo 11 Command Module, and the Albert Einstein Planetarium.

WEBSITE
starchild.gsfc.nasa.gov

Learn more about the Solar System, the universe, and more at NASA's Goddard Space Flight Center's kid-friendly website.

Photo Credits

FRONT COVER: Image creation by Iwona Usakiewicz/Andrij Borys Associates, Images used – Top: ©Antony McAuly/SS, Bottom: ©Steve Bronstein/GY, ©Deltev van Ravenswaay/GY; BACK COVER: ©Peter Jurik/DT; p 1: ©NASA; pp 2-3: ©NASA/T. Arai/University of Tokyo; pp 4-5: ©Ganna Poltoratska/DT; p 6 Top LtR: ©NASA, ESA, and the Hubble Heritage Team (STScI/AURA), ©NASA/JPL/University of Arizona, Middle LtR: ©NASA, ©By NASA / Bill Anders [Public domain], via Wikimedia Commons, ©NASA/Hubble, Bottom LtR: ©NASA's Solar Dynamics Observatory, ©NASA/MSFC/Aaron Kingery, ©NASA; p 7: Courtesy of Discovery Communications, LLC; pp 8-9 BG: ©Christos Georghiou/DT; p 9 TtB: ©Courtesy of Discovery Communications, LLC, ©Viktar Malyshchyts/SS; pp 10-11 BG: ©Pavlo Vakhrushev/DT; p 10 LtR: ©Enrique Gomez/DT, ©NASA; pp 12-13 BG: ©Bildagentur Zoonar GmbH/SS; p 12: ©Nelson Ikheafe/DT; pp 14-15 BG: ©peresanz/SS; pp 16-17 BG: ©Courtesy of Discovery Communications, LLC, TL: ©Tatyana Vyc/SS, BR: ©Roberto Rizzo/DT; pp 18-19 BG: All images: ©Keitikei/DT; pp 20-21 BG: All images: ©Keitikei/DT; pp 22-23 FR: ©Milagli/SS, Bottom LtR: ©SC, ©Royal Astronomical Society/SC, ©James Feliciano/DT, ©NASA; pp 24-25 BG: ©David Lloyd/DT, CL: ©Adele De Witte/DT, ©Neonriver/DT, ©Javier Larrea/age fotostock/SU, ©W. M. Keck Observatory, ©Dennis van de Water/SS; pp 26-27 BG: ©Icefront/DT; p 28 TtB: ©See page for author [Public domain or Public domain], via Wikimedia Commons, ©By Unknown Deutsch: Unbekannt English: Unknown Polski: Nieznany [Public domain], via Wikimedia Commons, ©By Eduard Ender († 1883) (http://cache.eb.com/eb/image?id=83677&rendTypeId=4) [Public domain], via Wikimedia Commons; p 29: ©LSkywalker/SS; pp 30-31 Top BG: ©oriontrail/SS, Circle images CL: ©AnikaNes/SS, ©Dmitri Maruta/DT, ©David Cabrera Navarro/DT, ©Annette Shaff/SS, ©Mohammed Anwarul Kabir Choudhury/DT; Bottom: ©Dmitrijs Mihejevs/SS; pp 32-33 BG: ©NASA, FR: ©Nepster/SS; p 32 TtB: ©Khellon/DT, ©Cgardinerphotos/DT; pp 34-35 BG: ©Biosphoto/SU, FL: ©Chad Baker/NASA, FR: ©Jerry Coli/DT; pp 36-37 Top LtR: ©LSkywalker/SS, ©KPG_Payless/SS, Bottom: ©NASA/Bill Dunford; pp 38-39 BG: ©Keith Tarrier/SS, ©Eclipse vectors: Alhovik/SS; pp 40-41 BG: ©Yuriy Kulik/SS; p 40: ©ESA/NASA/SOHO; p 41 TtB: ©Paladin12/SS, ©Melinda Fawver/SS, ©Laszlo66/SS; pp 42-43 BG: ©Vladimir Arndt/SS; p 42: ©NASA; p 43 Top: ©Brocreative/SS, ©Monkey Business Images/SS, Middle: ©photopixel/SS, ©etvulc/SS, Bottom: ©Naeblys/SS, ©Mopic/SS; pp 44-45 BG: ©Frozenmost/SS; p 44 TtB: ©NASA/SDO, ©solarseven/SS; p 45 TtB: ©NASA, ©National Oceanic and Atmospheric Administration/Department of Commerce, pp 46-47 BG: ©Loke Yek Mang/DT, Bottom LtR: ©NASA, ©Stocktrek Images/SU, ©NASA; p 47 TtB: ©NASA/Goddard Space Flight Center, ©Everett Historical/SS; p 48

Images: ©NASA; p 49 Top: ©By NASA [Public domain], via Wikimedia Commons, Center: ©By NASA [Public domain], via Wikimedia Commons, ©NASA, ©By NASA [Public domain], via Wikimedia Commons, Bottom LtR: ©By NASA [Public domain], via Wikimedia Commons, ©NASA; pp 50-51 BG: ©Tatyana Vyc/SS, p 50 LtR: ©By NASA [Public domain], via Wikimedia Commons, ©NASA; p 51 Images: ©NASA; pp 52-53 BG: ©NASA/SU; p 52 TtB: ©NASA, ©NASA/SU, ©By NASA [Public domain], via Wikimedia Commons; p 53 TtB: ©NASA Edgar D. Mitchell, ©NASA, ©NASA/SU; pp 54-55 BG: ©NASA; p 55 CL: ©NASA, ©NASA/Victor Zelentsov, ©NASA; pp 56-57 BG: ©Kwiktor/DT; pp 58-59 BG: ©shooarts/SS; p 58 Bottom: ©Jorge Salcedo; pp 60-61 BG: ©Jerry Lodriguss/SC, Bottom LtR: ©iryna1/SS, ©Thomas Murray [Public domain], via Wikimedia Commons, ©NASA Ames, ©NASA/JPL/Space Science Institute; p 61: ©Ben Cooper/SU; pp 62: ©Spencer Sutton/SC; p 63 TtB: ©NASA, ©Monica Schroeder/SC; p 64 TtB: ©Antony McAulay/SS, ©NASA/Johns Hopkins University Applied Physics Laboratory/Carnegie Institution of Washington; p 65 TtB: ©By NASA / Jet Propulsion Laboratory [Public domain], via Wikimedia Commons, ©NASA/SU; p 66: ©Antony McAulay/SS; p 67 TtB: ©Nomad/SU, ©Science and Society/SU; p 68: ©Antony McAulay/SS; p 69 Top: ©PhotoStockImage/SS, Bottom LtR: ©Courtesy of Discovery Communications, LLC, ©Alexkharkov/DT; pp 70-71 BG: ©U. Gernhoefer/SS, FL: ©Frenta/DT, FL: ©Pathastings/DT; pp 72-73 BG: ©Chatchai Kritsetsakul/SS, ©LSkywalker/SS; p 74: ©Antony McAulay/SS; p 75 CL: ©Science and Society/SU, ©NASA/SU, ©NASA/JPL/University of Arizona, ©NASA/JPL-Caltech/University of Arizona; pp 76-77 BG: ©Anton Watman; p 76 TtB: ©NASA/JPL-Caltech/MSSS, ©NASA/SC; p 77 TtB: ©NASA/SU, ©DiBiase et al/Journal of Geophyscial Research/2013 USGS/NASA Landsat; pp 78-79 BG: ©Edouard Coleman/SS; p 78: ©NASA/JPL-Caltech, Inset image: ©NASA/JPL-Caltech/Malin Space Science Systems; p 79 TtB: ©NASA/JPL-Caltech/Cornell/Arizona State Univ., ©NASA; p 80 TtB: ©Antony McAulay/SS, ©NASA; p 81 TtB: ©Tristan3D/SS, ©NASA; pp 82-83 BG: ©NASA/JPL/Space Science Institute, FL: ©Patrimonio Designs Limited/DT, FR: ©Georgios Kollidas/SS; p 84: ©Antony McAulay/SS; p 85 TtB: ©NASA/JPL-Caltech/Space Science Institute, ©NASA/JPL/University of Arizona; pp 86-87 BG: ©Nicku/DT; pp 88-89 FL: ©NASA/ESA/M. Showalter (SETI Institute), ©NASA/JPL; pp 90-91 FL TtB: ©NASA, ©NASA/JPL, FR: ©NASA Planetary Photojournal; pp 92-93 BG: ©Stefano Garau/SS; p 92 LtR: ©NASA/JPL, ©NASA; p 93 FL: ©NASA/JHU APL/SwRI, FR TtB: ©NASA/JHUAPL/SWRI, ©NASA/JHUAPL/SwRI; pp 94-95 BG: ©Sarah Barry/SS; p 94: ©Stocktrek Images/GY; p 95 TtB: ©By NASA [Public domain], via Wikimedia Commons, ©NASA, ©NASA-B. Ingalls; pp 96-97 BG: ©Phatthanit/SS, CL: ©NASA, ©NASA, ©NASA, ©See page for author [Public domain], via Wikimedia Commons, ©By NASA [Public domain], via Wikimedia Commons, ©NASA; pp 98-99 BG: ©By NASA [Public domain], via Wikimedia Commons, FL: ©Wisconsinart/DT, FL: ©By NASA/Robert Markowitz [Public domain], via Wikimedia Commons; pp 100-101 BG: ©Andrey

Armyagov/SS, CL: ©NASA, ©NASA, ©NASA Spinoff; pp 102-103 BG: ©IM_photo/SS; p 102 TtB: ©NASA/GRC, ©NASA, ©NASA; p 103 TtB: ©NASA/Emmett Given, ©NASA/BioServe, ©Danielle Anthony/NASA; pp 104-105 BG: ©ESO/C. Malin; pp 106-107 BG: ©Astrostar/SS, LtR: ©NASA/JPL-Caltech/UCLA/DLR/IDA, ©Derek Trott/DT, ©Courtesy of the NEAR Project (JHU/APL), ©NASA/JPL; pp 108-109 BG: ©4Max/SS; p 108: ©NASA/J.-C. Li; p 109 TtB: ©By NASA (NASA) [Public domain], via Wikimedia Commons, ©NASA; pp 110-111 BG: ©Mike Hollingshead/age fotostock/SU; p 111 TtB: ©NASA/JPL-Caltech/UCAL/MPS/DLR/IDA, ©Gunnar Assmy/SS, ©NASA/JPL-Caltech, ©Nikola Spasenoski/SS; pp 112-113 BG: ©turtix/SS; p 113 TtB: ©NASA-JSC, ©Discovery Communications, LLC; pp 114-115 BG: ©Manuel Ploetz/SS; p 114: ©NASA; p 115 CL: ©NASA, ©By National Aeronautics and Space Administration (NASA), Applied Physics Laboratory [Public domain], via Wikimedia Commons, ©NASA/JHUAPL/SwRI, ©SC; pp 116-117 BG: ©Rob Jones/DT, FL: ©NASA/JPL-Caltech, FR TtB: ©Suyerry/DT, ©By NASA, ESA, and H. Weaver and E. Smith (STScI) [Public domain], via Wikimedia Commons; pp 118-119 All images: ©SC; pp 120-121 BG: ©NASA, ESA, and the Hubble Heritage Team (STScI/AURA)-ESA/Hubble Collaboration; p 122: ©Designua/SS; p 123 TtB: ©NASA/ESA, ©NASA; pp 124-125: ©NASA and the Night Sky Network; pp 126-127 CL: ©Azstarman/DT, ©NASA, ESA, HEIC, and The Hubble Heritage Team (STScI/AURA), ©NASA/STScI Digitized Sky Survey/Noel Carboni, ©peresanz/SS, ©a. v. ley/SS; pp 128-129 BG: ©NASA/SU; p 128: ©Exactostock-1527/SU; pp 130-131 LtR: ©ESO/Digitized Sky Survey 2/Acknowledgement: Davide De Martin, ©ESA/Hubble & NASA; pp 132-133 BG: ©John Chumack/SC, LtR: ©John Chumack/SS, Constellation images: ©angelinast/SS; pp 134-135 CL: ©ESO/L. Calçada, ©NASA, ESA, and E. Sabbi/STScI, ©NASA, NOAO, and A. Rest (STScI); pp 136: ©Science and Society/SU; p 137 TtB: ©Yury Dmitrienko/SS, ©Vaclav Volrab/SS, ©exopixel/SS; pp 138: ©Markus Schieder/DT; p 139 TtB: ©NASA/JPL-Caltech/O. Krause (Steward Observatory), ©By nsf.gov [Public domain], via Wikimedia Commons; pp 140-141 CL: ©NASA/CXC/Univ. of Wisconsin-Madison/S. Heinz et. Al, ©NASA/CXC/SAO: X-ray; NASA/JPL-Caltech: Infrared, ©ESO/L. Calçada; pp 142-143 BG: ©NASA, LtR: ©NASA/CXC/Amherst College/D. Haggard et al, ©X-ray: NASA/CXC/SAO/D. Patnaude et al, Optical: ESO/VLT, Infrared: NASA/JPL/Caltech; pp 144-145 BG: ©Julian Baum/SC, FL: ©Spencer Sutton/SC; pp 146-147 BG and TR: ©fluidworkshop/SS, BR: ©Cathy Keifer/SS; pp 148-149 CL: ©Jim Sugar/CB, ©WitthayaP/SS, ©Nataliya Evmenenko/DT, ©Oleg Zhukov/DT, ©curraheeshutter/SS, ©Nightman1965/SS; pp 150-151 LtR: ©By SKA Project Development Office and Swinburne Astronomy Productions [CC BY-SA 3.0 (http://creativecommons.org/licenses/by-sa/3.0) or GFDL (http://www.gnu.org/copyleft/fdl.html)], via Wikimedia Commons, ©By NASA (https://mix.msfc.nasa.gov/abstracts.php?p=330) [Public domain], via Wikimedia Commons, ©X-ray: NASA/CXC/ Univ. of Michigan/A.E.Jaskot, Optical: NOAO/CTIO/MCELS, ©By Photo credit: NASA/Jim Grossmann [Public domain], via Wikimedia

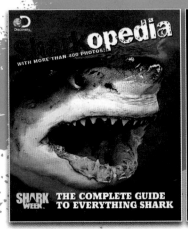
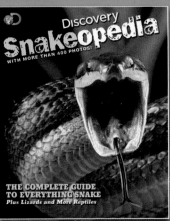